THE TECHNOLOGICAL SINGULARITY

ARE WE READY FOR HIGHER AI?

DAVID SANDUA

"Artificial intelligence is the new electricity.
It will transform every industry, but we must manage its risks".

Andrew Ng - AI researcher and co-founder of Google Brain

INDEX

8

9

I. INTRODUCTION

Artificial Intelligence (AI) has made significant strides in recent years, with advancements in machine learning and deep neural networks pushing the boundaries of what technology can achieve. These developments have led to discussions about the idea of the technological singularity, a hypothetical event where AI surpasses human intelligence, potentially leading to profound societal changes. As we move closer to this potential turning point, it is crucial to consider the implications of higher AI. From revolutionizing industries like healthcare and automotive to raising concerns about job displacement and ethical dilemmas, the impact of advanced AI technology is far-reaching and complex. The transformative power of AI is already evident in various sectors, with applications ranging from autonomous vehicles to medical diagnostics. While these innovations offer tremendous benefits such as improved efficiency and accuracy, they also raise important questions about privacy, security, and equitable access to technology. As AI systems become more sophisticated and autonomous, the need for ethical guidelines and regulatory frameworks becomes increasingly urgent. In navigating this rapidly evolving landscape, it is essential for policymakers, industry leaders, and researchers to collaborate in shaping a future that balances innovation with social responsibility. As society grapples with the implications of higher AI, there is a growing realization of the need for comprehensive strategies to prepare for this technological shift. This includes reevaluating education and workforce training programs to equip individuals with the skills needed to thrive in a digital world increasingly shaped by AI. Addressing the potential economic repercussions of automation and job displacement requires proactive measures to ensure a smooth transition. By fostering dialogue and proactive planning, we can better anticipate the challenges and opportunities that come with advancing AI capabilities, ultimately empowering us to shape a future that benefits all members of society.

Definition of Technological Singularity

Continuing the exploration of the technological singularity, it is crucial to understand the concepts implications for society. As AI continues to advance at an exponential pace, there is a growing concern about the potential consequences of reaching a point where AI surpasses human intelligence. This could lead to a fundamental shift in how we live and work, impacting everything from job markets to geopolitical dynamics. The prospect of machines making decisions that are beyond human comprehension raises ethical dilemmas and challenges the very essence of what it means to be human. As we move closer to the singularity, it becomes imperative for us to critically assess our values and priorities as a society to ensure that we are prepared for the changes that lie ahead. The definition of technological singularity also encompasses the idea of a transformative event that could reshape the course of human history. It implies a moment when AI becomes self-improving, leading to an intelligence explosion that could radically alter the fabric of society. This potential for rapid and unpredictable change poses significant risks as well as opportunities. The exponential growth of AI capabilities could revolutionize fields such as healthcare, transportation, and communication, offering immense benefits to humanity. It also raises concerns about the concentration of power in the hands of AI systems and the potential for unintended consequences. Balancing the promise of technological progress with the need for responsible innovation is a critical challenge that must be addressed as we approach the singularity. The concept of the technological singularity underscores the need for proactive measures to ensure that AI development aligns with human values and aspirations. As we venture into uncharted territory where machines may surpass human cognitive abilities, the ethical and regulatory frameworks that govern AI become increasingly important. Establishing guidelines for the responsible development and deployment of AI systems is essential to mitigate risks and maximize the benefits of advanced technology. By fostering a culture of collaboration between humans and machines, we can harness the full potential of AI while safeguarding against potential pitfalls. It is through thoughtful planning and collective action that we can navigate the complexities of the singularity and pave the way for a future where humans and AI can coexist harmoniously.

Brief history of AI development

The development of AI can be traced back to the mid-20th century, with the inception of the first neural networks and early computer programs designed to perform complex tasks. One of the key milestones in AI history was the creation of the Dartmouth Conference in 1956, where the term AI was coined, and researchers laid out a vision for creating machines that could think and learn like humans. Throughout the following decades, AI saw periods of rapid advancement and stagnation, influenced by factors such as funding, computing power, and shifts in research focus. In the 1990s, machine learning algorithms gained prominence, paving the way for more sophisticated AI systems capable of recognizing patterns and making decisions based on data. As computational capabilities increased and data became more abundant, AI research experienced a resurgence in the early 21st century. Breakthroughs in deep learning, a subset of machine learning focused on neural networks with multiple layers, revolutionized the field by enabling computers to process vast amounts of data and extract meaningful insights. This led to the development of AI applications ranging from image and speech recognition to autonomous vehicles and medical diagnosis systems. The integration of AI into various industries has reshaped business operations and consumer experiences, demonstrating the potential for these technologies to drive innovation and efficiency at scale. Looking ahead, the trajectory of AI development is poised to continue its upward trend, with investments pouring into research labs and companies around the world. As AI systems become more sophisticated and autonomous, questions around ethical considerations, accountability, and the potential for unintended consequences have come to the forefront. It is crucial for policymakers, industry leaders, and the public to engage in conversations about the responsible deployment of AI, ensuring that the benefits of these technologies are maximized while safeguarding against potential risks. As we stand on the cusp of a new era of AI-driven innovation, it is essential to approach these advancements with caution and mindfulness to steer towards a future where AI works in harmony with human society.

Thesis statement

In considering the implications of the technological singularity, one cannot overlook the significance of the thesis statement that guides the analysis of this complex concept. The thesis statement serves as the foundation on which the entire argument is built, providing a clear and concise articulation of the main point or central claim being made. In the case of the technological singularity, the thesis statement may assert that advancements in AI are rapidly approaching a point where machines will surpass human intelligence, leading to profound societal transformations. This statement not only sets the direction for the discussion but also helps to establish the scope and focus of the essay, ensuring that all subsequent points are aligned with the overarching argument. The thesis statement plays a crucial role in shaping the structure of the essay, helping to organize the content in a logical and coherent manner. By clearly articulating the main argument or perspective being advanced, the thesis statement provides a roadmap for the reader, indicating what to expect in terms of the analysis and evidence that will be presented. This structuring function is particularly important in complex topics such as the technological singularity, where a multitude of ideas and perspectives must be synthesized and integrated to form a cohesive and persuasive argument. Without a strong thesis statement to guide the way, the essay risks losing focus and coherence, ultimately undermining the effectiveness of the analysis. The thesis statement serves as a linchpin in the exploration of the technological singularity, offering a concise and insightful summary of the central argument being advanced. By clearly articulating the main point or claim of the essay, the thesis statement provides a framework for the analysis, guiding the discussion and ensuring a logical and coherent progression of ideas. In this way, the thesis statement not only facilitates a deeper understanding of the topic but also enhances the overall persuasiveness and impact of the essay. As such, constructing a robust and well-crafted thesis statement is essential in grappling with complex issues such as the technological singularity, enabling a more focused and systematic examination of the challenges and opportunities presented by advanced artificial intelligence.

II. CURRENT STATE OF AI

In the current state of AI, researchers and developers are pushing boundaries with advancements in machine learning algorithms and deep neural networks. These breakthroughs are revolutionizing various industries, leading to increased efficiency, accuracy, and automation. AI is being used in healthcare for diagnostic purposes, enabling more precise and timely treatment plans. Similarly, in the automotive industry, self-driving technology is redefining transportation and safety standards. These applications demonstrate the potential of AI to enhance human capabilities and improve quality of life. The current state of AI raises important questions about the ethical and regulatory considerations surrounding its development and deployment. As AI systems become more sophisticated and autonomous, concerns about bias, privacy, and accountability have come to the forefront. It is essential to establish guidelines and frameworks that ensure AI technologies are developed and used in a responsible and transparent manner. By addressing these ethical challenges, society can harness the full potential of AI while mitigating potential risks and unintended consequences. Looking ahead, society must assess its readiness to embrace higher AI technologies and their implications. This includes evaluating the impact of automation on the workforce and economy, as well as the need for education and training programs to equip individuals with the skills to navigate a rapidly changing technological landscape. As we move towards the technological singularity, it is vital to foster a collaborative relationship between humans and AI, emphasizing the importance of ethical decision-making and responsible innovation. By preparing for the challenges and opportunities that higher AI presents, we can ensure a more sustainable and inclusive future for all.

Types of AI systems

Moving beyond machine learning systems and deep neural networks, another type of AI system worth exploring is expert systems. Expert systems are designed to mimic the decision-making processes of a human expert in a specific domain. These systems can store vast amounts of knowledge and use reasoning mechanisms to provide insights or make recommendations. By leveraging expert systems, industries can benefit from consistent and reliable decision-making, especially in complex or specialized fields such as medicine or finance. In contrast to expert systems, fuzzy logic AI systems operate on the principle of approximate reasoning rather than strict binary logic. These systems are adept at handling uncertainties and imprecise information, making them valuable in situations where clear-cut decisions are not feasible. Fuzzy logic AI systems have been applied in various areas, including control systems for appliances and vehicles, optimizing performance based on input variables that may not always be black and white. Evolutionary computation AI systems take inspiration from biological evolution to solve complex problems through iterative improvement and selection processes. These systems use algorithms such as genetic algorithms and genetic programming to generate solutions based on the principles of mutation, fitness evaluation, and survival of the fittest. Evolutionary computation AI systems have shown promise in optimizing processes, designing products, and even creating new algorithms, offering a unique approach to problem-solving that mimics natural selection and evolution.

Applications of AI in various fields

In the field of healthcare, AI is revolutionizing diagnostics and personalized medicine. Machine learning algorithms are being used to analyze medical images, detect patterns, and predict diseases with high accuracy. This has resulted in faster and more precise diagnoses, leading to better patient outcomes. AI-driven platforms are enabling doctors to tailor treatment plans based on individual genetic makeups, optimizing the effectiveness of interventions. The integration of AI in healthcare has the potential to significantly reduce healthcare costs, improve patient care, and even save lives. Another area where AI is making a significant impact is in the automotive industry. Autonomous vehicles, powered by AI technologies such as computer vision and natural language processing, are poised to revolutionize transportation. These self-driving cars can navigate traffic, anticipate road conditions, and make split-second decisions that prioritize safety. By reducing human error, AI-driven vehicles have the potential to reduce accidents, increase efficiency, and lower transportation costs. As the automotive industry continues to invest in AI research and development, we can expect to see a rapid transformation in how we commute and travel. The financial sector is also embracing AI to enhance customer experiences and streamline processes. AI-powered chatbots and virtual assistants are being used to provide personalized financial advice, improve fraud detection, and optimize investment portfolios. By analyzing vast amounts of data in real-time, AI systems can identify trends, risks, and opportunities that humans may overlook. This not only benefits financial institutions in terms of efficiency and profitability but also enhances customer satisfaction by delivering tailored solutions. As AI continues to evolve, we can anticipate further innovations in the financial sector that will reshape the way we interact with money and investments.

Ethical considerations in AI development

Ethical considerations play a crucial role in the development of artificial intelligence. As AI systems become increasingly sophisticated, questions arise about the implications of their decisions and actions. Issues such as bias in algorithms, data privacy, and accountability are central to the ethical discourse surrounding AI. Biased training data can lead to discriminatory outcomes, reinforcing existing inequalities in society. It is essential for developers and policymakers to address these ethical concerns proactively to ensure that AI technologies are used responsibly and in the best interests of all stakeholders. Transparency and explainability are key components of ethical AI development. As AI systems become more autonomous and make decisions that impact human lives, it is essential for these systems to provide clear explanations for their actions. This not only fosters trust between humans and AI but also allows for better oversight and accountability. Ensuring that AI systems operate in a transparent and interpretable manner is essential for mitigating risks and addressing unintended consequences. By prioritizing transparency and explainability in AI development, developers can build systems that are ethically sound and aligned with societal values. The establishment of robust regulatory frameworks is essential to guide the development and deployment of AI technologies. Regulations can help set standards for ethical AI design, ensuring that AI systems operate within legal and ethical boundaries. By implementing regulations that mandate ethical considerations in AI development, policymakers can safeguard against potential harms and promote the responsible use of AI. A collaborative approach involving industry, academia, and government is needed to create a cohesive regulatory framework that balances technological advancement with ethical considerations. A comprehensive regulatory framework can support the responsible and ethical development of AI, benefiting society as a whole.

III. ADVANTAGES OF HIGHER AI

One of the significant advantages of higher AI lies in its potential to revolutionize the healthcare industry. With advanced AI systems capable of processing vast amounts of data and identifying patterns, medical professionals can make more accurate diagnoses and provide personalized treatment plans for patients. As a result, the overall quality of healthcare services is expected to improve, leading to better patient outcomes and reduced healthcare costs. AI-powered medical devices and robots can assist in surgeries, monitor patients vital signs, and even dispense medication, enhancing the efficiency and effectiveness of healthcare delivery. The adoption of higher AI in the automotive sector offers numerous benefits, particularly in the realm of autonomous vehicles. By integrating AI technologies, self-driving cars can navigate complex road conditions, reduce traffic accidents, and optimize transportation systems. These advancements not only enhance safety on the roads but also improve the overall driving experience for individuals. AI-enabled predictive maintenance systems can help prevent vehicle breakdowns and decrease maintenance costs for fleet owners. Higher AI has the potential to transform the automotive industry by making transportation safer, more efficient, and environmentally friendly. In addition to healthcare and automotive industries, higher AI offers advantages in various other sectors, such as finance, agriculture, and cybersecurity. In finance, AI-powered algorithms can analyze market trends, detect fraudulent activities, and provide personalized investment recommendations to clients. In agriculture, AI-driven technologies can optimize crop yields, reduce water usage, and increase the efficiency of farming operations. In cybersecurity, AI systems can detect and respond to cyber threats in real-time, strengthening the defense mechanisms of organizations against potential attacks. By leveraging the benefits of higher AI across different industries, businesses and societies can unlock new opportunities for growth, innovation, and sustainability.

Increased efficiency and productivity

Increased efficiency and productivity are key drivers behind the advancement of AI technologies. By integrating AI systems into various industries, businesses can streamline processes, optimize resource allocation, and enhance overall performance. In manufacturing, AI-powered robotics can improve production output and quality while reducing costs and time. This not only benefits companies by boosting their competitiveness but also contributes to economic growth at a larger scale. AI algorithms can analyze vast amounts of data in real-time, identifying patterns and trends that humans may overlook, leading to more informed decision-making and strategic planning. In the realm of healthcare, the potential for increased efficiency through AI is particularly promising. Diagnostic tools powered by AI can process medical images, lab results, and patient data with unprecedented speed and accuracy, aiding healthcare professionals in making accurate diagnoses and treatment plans. AI can also automate routine administrative tasks, allowing healthcare staff to focus more on patient care. By enhancing the efficiency of healthcare systems, AI has the potential to improve patient outcomes, reduce medical errors, and lower healthcare costs. It is essential to establish ethical guidelines and regulations to ensure that AI technologies are used responsibly and in the best interest of patients and society at large. The integration of AI technologies holds great promise for increasing efficiency and productivity across various sectors. By harnessing the power of AI to automate tasks, analyze data, and make informed decisions, businesses and industries can achieve higher levels of performance and competitiveness. As AI becomes more pervasive, it is crucial to address ethical considerations, ensure transparency, and safeguard against potential risks such as job displacement and algorithmic biases. A balanced approach that combines technological innovation with ethical responsibility will be key to realizing the full potential of AI in improving efficiency and productivity while fostering a more equitable and sustainable future.

Potential for solving complex problems

Moving forward, the potential for solving complex problems through higher AI is immense. With advanced machine learning algorithms and deep neural networks, AI systems can analyze vast amounts of data, identifying patterns and insights that would be impossible for humans to discover on their own. This capability is already revolutionizing industries such as healthcare, where AI can assist in diagnosis and treatment planning, improving patient outcomes and saving lives. In the automotive sector, AI-powered autonomous vehicles are paving the way for safer and more efficient transportation systems. By harnessing the power of AI, we can tackle challenges that were previously insurmountable, ushering in a new era of innovation and progress. The ability of AI to handle complex problems extends beyond specific industries to areas like climate change, cybersecurity, and urban planning. With AIs computational speed and analytical prowess, we can develop more effective strategies for mitigating the impacts of global warming, enhancing cybersecurity measures to protect sensitive data, and optimizing urban infrastructure for sustainable growth. As AI continues to advance, its problem-solving capabilities will only improve, providing valuable insights and solutions to some of the most pressing challenges facing society today. By leveraging AI technology, we can address complex problems with greater efficiency and effectiveness, driving progress and innovation in fields across the board. The potential for solving complex problems through higher AI is a testament to the transformative power of advanced technology. As AI continues to evolve and improve, its problem-solving capabilities will only become more sophisticated, enabling us to tackle challenges that were once thought to be beyond our reach. As we harness the power of AI to address complex problems, it is essential to prioritize ethical considerations and ensure that these technologies are used responsibly. By approaching the development and deployment of AI with caution and foresight, we can maximize its benefits while minimizing potential risks. By embracing AI as a tool for solving complex problems, we can pave the way for a more innovative, efficient, and prosperous future for humanity.

Advancements in healthcare and science

Advancements in healthcare and science have been propelled by groundbreaking technologies such as artificial intelligence. In healthcare, AI is revolutionizing patient care with predictive analytics, robotic surgery, and personalized treatment plans. Machine learning algorithms can analyze vast amounts of data to identify patterns that humans might miss, leading to more accurate diagnoses and tailored interventions. AI-powered tools like wearable devices and telemedicine platforms are enhancing access to healthcare services, especially in remote areas. The integration of AI in scientific research has also accelerated the pace of discovery and innovation. AI algorithms can sift through massive datasets to identify potential drug candidates, predict disease outbreaks, and optimize experimental protocols. This has significantly reduced the time and cost associated with drug development and clinical trials. AI-driven simulations and modeling have expanded our understanding of complex biological processes, paving the way for new therapies and interventions. Despite the tremendous potential of AI in healthcare and science, ethical considerations loom large. Issues such as data privacy, bias in algorithmic decision-making, and the impact on jobs and human roles in these fields need to be carefully addressed. Striking a balance between technological advancement and ethical responsibility is crucial to ensuring that the benefits of AI are harnessed while mitigating potential risks. By fostering collaboration between technologists, ethicists, policymakers, and healthcare professionals, we can navigate the challenges and opportunities presented by AI in healthcare and science, ultimately leading to a more equitable and sustainable future.

IV. CHALLENGES OF HIGHER AI

One of the major challenges posed by higher AI is the potential loss of human control over advanced autonomous systems. As AI continues to progress towards the singularity, it becomes increasingly difficult for humans to anticipate and understand the decisions made by these systems. This lack of transparency can lead to unintended consequences and ethical dilemmas, especially in critical domains such as healthcare, finance, and national security. Without the ability to fully comprehend the reasoning behind AI-generated outcomes, humans may struggle to maintain oversight and accountability, raising concerns about the potential for AI systems to act independently and even in contradiction to human values and goals. The rise of higher AI presents significant challenges in terms of data privacy and security. As AI systems become more sophisticated and autonomous, they rely on vast amounts of data to learn and make decisions. This raises concerns about the potential misuse or mishandling of sensitive information, especially given the increasing frequency of data breaches and cyberattacks. In a world where AI is deeply integrated into various aspects of society, safeguarding personal data and ensuring the security of AI systems becomes paramount. Without robust measures in place to protect data privacy and cybersecurity, the proliferation of higher AI may inadvertently expose individuals and organizations to unforeseen risks and vulnerabilities. Another crucial challenge of higher AI is the potential for exacerbating societal inequalities and economic disparities. While AI has the power to revolutionize industries and drive economic growth, it also has the capacity to disrupt traditional job markets and displace human workers. As automation and AI technologies become more prevalent, certain jobs may become obsolete, leading to widespread unemployment and economic instability. Addressing these challenges requires proactive measures to retrain and reskill the workforce, as well as developing policies that promote inclusive growth and equitable access to the benefits of AI innovation. By acknowledging and actively mitigating the social impacts of higher AI, we can work towards a more sustainable and equitable future where technological advancement benefits society as a whole.

Job displacement and economic implications
As AI continues to advance, job displacement becomes an increasingly pressing issue with profound economic implications. The automation of tasks previously performed by humans has the potential to disrupt industries on a large scale, leading to widespread unemployment and economic instability. As machines become more efficient and cost-effective than human workers, businesses may opt to replace their employees with automated systems to reduce expenses and increase productivity. This shift towards automation could result in a significant portion of the workforce being displaced, creating challenges for individuals seeking reemployment and for the overall economy. The mass displacement of workers due to AI-driven automation poses a range of economic challenges that must be addressed. Not only does job loss impact individuals and families on a personal level, but it also has broader implications for society as a whole. The loss of income and purchasing power for a large segment of the population can lead to decreased consumer

27

spending, which in turn affects businesses and economic growth. The unequal distribution of the benefits of AI innovation may exacerbate income inequality, creating social tensions and further destabilizing the economy. It is essential for policymakers and business leaders to proactively address these challenges through strategic planning and targeted interventions to mitigate the negative economic impacts of job displacement. As we navigate the complexities of job displacement in the age of AI, it is crucial to consider proactive measures to address these economic implications effectively. Investing in education and training programs that equip individuals with the skills needed for the evolving job market is essential to help workers transition to new roles and industries. Establishing policies that support job creation in emerging fields that complement AI technologies can help offset the negative effects of automation on employment. By fostering a culture of innovation and adaptability, we can harness the potential of AI to drive economic growth and create new opportunities for individuals in the workforce. Embracing a forward-thinking approach to job displacement can lead to a more resilient economy that thrives in the face of technological change.

Ethical dilemmas in AI decision-making

In the realm of AI decision-making, ethical dilemmas often arise due to the complexity of the tasks assigned to intelligent systems. One major concern is the issue of bias in AI algorithms, where the data used to train these systems may inadvertently perpetuate discriminatory practices. This can result in biased decision-making processes that have real-world consequences, such as in hiring practices or judicial sentencing. Addressing these biases requires careful examination of the data inputs, as well as ongoing monitoring and adjustments to ensure fairness and equity in AI-driven decisions. The transparency of AI decision-making processes is crucial in fostering trust among users and stakeholders. The opacity of many AI algorithms raises concerns about accountability and the ability to understand the rationale behind certain decisions. Without transparency, it becomes challenging to identify errors or biases in the system, leading to potential harm or injustice. Establishing standards for transparency in AI decision-making, including clear explanations of how decisions are reached, can help mitigate these risks and build confidence in the technology. The question of moral agency in AI decision-making poses a philosophical challenge. As AI systems become more advanced and autonomous, the issue of who is responsible for the decisions made by these machines becomes increasingly complex. Should developers, users, or the AI itself be held accountable for the outcomes of its decisions? This dilemma requires a reevaluation of ethical frameworks and legal systems to accommodate the unique characteristics of AI and ensure that responsibility is assigned appropriately. Finding a balance between innovation and accountability is essential in navigating the ethical challenges of AI decision-making.

Security risks and potential misuse of AI technology

The potential misuse of AI technology poses significant security risks that must not be overlooked. As AI systems become more sophisticated, they may be vulnerable to cyber attacks or malicious manipulation. Hackers could exploit weaknesses in AI algorithms to cause disruptions in critical systems such as healthcare or transportation. The use of AI in surveillance and monitoring raises concerns about privacy violations and mass data collection without proper consent. These security risks highlight the importance of robust cybersecurity measures and ethical guidelines to safeguard against potential misuse of AI technology. In addition to external threats, there are also internal risks associated with the deployment of AI systems. Biases embedded in AI algorithms could result in discriminatory outcomes, particularly in sensitive areas such as hiring practices or criminal justice. The lack of transparency in AI decision-making processes raises concerns about accountability and the ability to challenge potentially harmful decisions. Addressing these internal risks requires a comprehensive approach that involves auditing AI systems for biases, promoting diversity in AI development teams, and establishing clear protocols for oversight and accountability. The security risks and potential misuse of AI technology underscore the need for a holistic approach to the development and deployment of advanced AI systems. By integrating cybersecurity measures, ethical guidelines, and proactive measures to address biases and promote transparency, society can mitigate the risks associated with AI while maximizing its benefits. It is essential for policymakers, researchers, and industry leaders to collaborate in establishing a regulatory framework that promotes responsible AI development and usage, ensuring that technology serves humanity while upholding ethical standards and protecting against potential security threats.

V. HUMAN-AI INTERACTION

In the realm of human-AI interaction, one crucial aspect to consider is the development of trust between individuals and AI systems. Trust is fundamental for any successful collaborative effort, and this applies to the interaction between humans and AI as well. Research has shown that users are more likely to follow AI recommendations and accept decisions when they trust the system. This highlights the importance of designing AI systems that are transparent, explainable, and reliable, fostering a sense of trust among users. Building trust in AI can lead to more effective decision-making processes and increased acceptance of AI technologies in various domains. The issue of accountability in human-AI interaction is a complex but essential consideration. As AI systems become more autonomous and make decisions that impact individuals and society as a whole, the question of who is responsible for the outcome of these decisions becomes critical. Establishing clear lines of accountability in AI development and deployment is crucial to ensure that ethical and legal standards are upheld. This involves defining roles and responsibilities for developers, users, and regulatory bodies, as well as implementing mechanisms for oversight and redress in case of errors or malfunctions. By addressing the issue of accountability proactively, we can mitigate potential risks associated with human-AI interaction and promote responsible AI governance. The concept of reciprocity in human-AI interaction adds another layer of complexity to the dynamic relationship between humans and artificial intelligence. Reciprocity refers to the mutual exchange of actions or behaviors between two parties, based on a sense of fairness and cooperation. In the context of AI, reciprocity involves designing systems that not only respond to human input but also anticipate, adapt, and collaborate with users to achieve common goals. By fostering a sense of reciprocity in human-AI interaction, we can enhance the overall user experience, promote engagement with AI technologies, and cultivate a more harmonious relationship between humans and intelligent machines. This emphasizes the need for a human-centered approach to AI design and development, where the principles of reciprocity and collaboration are at the forefront of creating beneficial and sustainable interactions.

Importance of human-AI collaboration

The importance of human-AI collaboration cannot be overstated when considering the ethical implications of advanced technologies. As AI systems become more sophisticated, the potential for bias and discrimination in decision-making processes increases. Human oversight and input are crucial to ensure that AI algorithms are fair and just, reflecting societal values and standards. By working together, humans and AI can create more ethically sound systems that promote equality and justice, rather than perpetuating existing biases. This collaboration also enables a deeper understanding of how AI operates, allowing for better regulation and governance of these powerful technologies. Human-AI collaboration enhances creativity and innovation in problem-solving. While AI excels at processing large amounts of data and identifying patterns, humans excel at thinking outside the box, connecting disparate ideas, and coming up with innovative solutions. By combining the strengths of both humans and AI, we can tackle complex challenges more effectively and generate new ideas that may not have been possible otherwise. This synergy fosters a dynamic and adaptive approach to problem-solving, driving progress and innovation across various industries and fields. The symbiotic relationship between humans and AI holds immense potential for shaping a future that benefits society as a whole. Collaboration between humans and AI is essential to harness the strengths of both parties, ensuring that technological advancements align with ethical values, foster creativity, and drive innovation. By understanding the significance of human-AI collaboration and actively engaging in it, we can navigate the complexities of the technological singularity and create a future where AI complements human capabilities, rather than supplanting them. This partnership is key to realizing the full potential of AI while safeguarding the well-being and prosperity of humanity.

Enhancing user experience through AI

In addition to revolutionizing industries, AI has the potential to greatly enhance user experience across various platforms. By leveraging machine learning algorithms, companies can personalize their services to cater to individual preferences and behaviors. E-commerce websites can recommend products based on past purchases, creating a more tailored shopping experience for users. This level of customization not only increases user satisfaction but also boosts engagement and loyalty. AI can analyze user feedback and interactions in real-time to make instant adjustments, ensuring a seamless and intuitive experience. AI-powered chatbots and virtual assistants have become essential tools for improving customer service. These intelligent systems can efficiently handle inquiries, provide relevant information, and even offer troubleshooting solutions. By incorporating natural language processing and sentiment analysis, these bots can understand and respond to human emotions, enhancing communication and problem-solving. The result is a more efficient and satisfying interaction for users, leading to increased brand trust and loyalty. AI can streamline processes such as online transactions, making them faster and more secure, ultimately enhancing the overall user experience. The integration of AI technologies into user interfaces has the potential to revolutionize the way individuals interact with digital platforms. By harnessing the power of AI, companies can create more personalized, efficient, and intuitive experiences for their users. This not only benefits consumers by providing tailored services and improved customer support but also drives business growth and competitiveness. As AI continues to evolve and advance, it will be crucial for organizations to adapt to these technological changes in order to stay ahead in the increasingly competitive market landscape. Enhancing user experience through AI holds immense potential for transforming the digital landscape and shaping the future of customer interaction.

Psychological impact of AI integration in daily life

The psychological impact of integrating AI into daily life is a complex phenomenon that is still being studied. One of the main concerns is the potential loss of human connection and empathy as people rely more on AI for tasks that used to require human interaction. In healthcare, AI systems can provide diagnoses and treatment recommendations based on data analysis, but they lack the emotional intelligence and understanding that a human healthcare provider can offer. This shift towards automation may lead to a sense of detachment and isolation, impacting individuals mental well-being. The increasing presence of AI in daily life raises questions about trust and reliance on technology. As people become more dependent on AI for decision-making and problem-solving, there is a risk of erosion in critical thinking skills and personal agency. Individuals may start to defer to AI systems for choices both big and small, without critically evaluating the information or outcomes. This overreliance on AI could potentially lead to a loss of control over ones own life, causing feelings of powerlessness and anxiety as individuals feel disconnected from their own decision-making processes. The integration of AI into daily life may also lead to concerns about privacy and security, amplifying fears of surveillance and data manipulation. With AI systems collecting massive amounts of personal data to tailor services and products, there is a heightened risk of breaches and misuse of sensitive information. This constant monitoring and data analysis can create a feeling of intrusion and vulnerability, affecting individuals sense of autonomy and self-determination. The psychological impact of living in a world where AI is ubiquitous is multifaceted, touching on issues of trust, control, and privacy that can shape individuals mental health and well-being in profound ways.

VI. REGULATORY FRAMEWORK FOR AI

The establishment of a comprehensive regulatory framework for AI is imperative to address the ethical concerns surrounding the development and deployment of advanced technologies. This framework should entail clear guidelines on data privacy, algorithm transparency, and accountability for AI systems. By defining these parameters, stakeholders can ensure that AI systems are designed and utilized in a responsible manner, minimizing the potential risks associated with their use. Such regulations can foster public trust in AI technologies, which is essential for widespread adoption and acceptance in society. Without a robust regulatory framework, there is a heightened risk of misuse or unintended consequences arising from the unchecked advancement of AI. The regulatory framework for AI must be adaptive and responsive to the rapid pace of technological innovation. As AI systems continue to evolve and integrate into various sectors of society, the regulatory landscape must be flexible enough to accommodate emerging challenges and developments. This requires ongoing collaboration between policymakers, industry experts, and ethicists to ensure that regulations remain relevant and effective in guiding the responsible development of AI. International cooperation is essential to harmonize regulatory standards across borders, facilitating the ethical use of AI on a global scale. By fostering a dynamic regulatory environment, we can promote innovation while safeguarding against potential risks associated with the unchecked proliferation of AI technologies. The regulatory framework for AI plays a pivotal role in shaping the future trajectory of technological advancement and ensuring that AI remains a force for good in society. By establishing clear guidelines and standards for the ethical development and deployment of AI systems, we can mitigate risks, promote transparency, and foster public trust in these transformative technologies. A flexible and collaborative approach to regulation is necessary to accommodate the rapid evolution of AI and address emerging challenges effectively. As we stand on the brink of the technological singularity, it is crucial that we prioritize the implementation of a robust regulatory framework to guide the responsible integration of AI into our lives and ensure that its benefits are realized in a manner that aligns with our values and aspirations as a society.

Current AI regulations and policies

In the realm of AI regulations and policies, there is an ongoing debate about how to balance innovation with ethical considerations. Current frameworks are grappling with the challenge of keeping pace with the rapid advancements in technology, particularly in the field of artificial intelligence. As AI systems become more sophisticated and autonomous, there is a growing need for clear guidelines on issues such as accountability, transparency, and bias mitigation. Policymakers must navigate the complex landscape of AI development to ensure that these technologies are used responsibly and for the benefit of society as a whole. International cooperation is crucial to establish common standards and norms that govern the ethical deployment of AI on a global scale. One of the key aspects of current AI regulations and policies is the focus on data privacy and security. As AI systems rely heavily on vast amounts of data to function effectively, there are concerns about how this data is collected, stored, and used. Regulations such as the General Data Protection Regulation (GDPR) in Europe aim to safeguard individual privacy rights and hold organizations accountable for how they handle personal data. Policies around cybersecurity are becoming increasingly important as the threat of data breaches and cyber attacks looms large. As AI technology continues to evolve, it is essential for regulations to adapt and address these evolving challenges to ensure that data is protected and that individuals rights are upheld. In the context of ethical considerations, policies around AI must also address issues of algorithmic bias and discrimination. AI systems are only as good as the data they are trained on, and if that data is biased, it can lead to discriminatory outcomes. Regulations need to account for these biases and ensure that AI systems are designed and implemented in a way that promotes fairness and equality. There is a growing recognition of the importance of explainability in AI systems, meaning that algorithms should be transparent and provide clear reasoning for their decisions. This transparency is essential for building trust in AI technology and ensuring that it is used in a way that aligns with societal values and norms. By developing comprehensive regulations and policies that address these ethical considerations, we can harness the full potential of AI while mitigating its risks and ensuring that it benefits all members of society.

Need for international cooperation in AI governance

The complexity of AI systems necessitates a collaborative effort on a global scale to establish comprehensive governance. With AI transcending borders, the need for international cooperation becomes paramount in addressing issues such as data privacy, cybersecurity, and algorithmic bias. Without unified regulations and standards, the development and deployment of AI technologies could lead to disparate outcomes and ethical dilemmas. By working together, countries can establish guidelines that foster innovation while upholding ethical principles and safeguarding individual rights. International cooperation in AI governance can also prevent a race to the bottom where countries prioritize technological advancements at the expense of ethical considerations. The interconnected nature of the digital world underscores the importance of harmonizing AI policies to ensure consistency and coherence. Without a unified approach to AI governance, discrepancies in regulations could create loopholes that allow unethical practices to flourish. By fostering collaboration among nations, a framework can be established to address common challenges and mitigate the risks associated with AI advancement. International cooperation can also facilitate information sharing and best practices, enabling countries to learn from each others experiences and adopt strategies that promote responsible AI development. Through collaboration, the global community can collectively shape the trajectory of AI innovation towards a more beneficial and sustainable future. The intersection of AI with critical domains such as healthcare, finance, and transportation underscores the need for unified governance to address sector-specific challenges. As AI becomes integral to various industries, a cohesive regulatory framework can provide clarity and guidance on how to navigate the complex landscape of AI applications. International cooperation in AI governance can also foster trust and credibility among stakeholders, assuring consumers and businesses that AI technologies are deployed ethically and responsibly. By establishing common norms and standards, countries can proactively address emerging issues and ensure that AI enhances societal well-being while minimizing potential harms. Collaboration in AI governance is essential to harnessing the full potential of AI while safeguarding the interests of humanity.

Balancing innovation with ethical AI development

In the race towards achieving higher levels of artificial intelligence, the delicate balance between innovation and ethical considerations must be carefully maintained. As AI technologies continue to advance at a rapid pace, the potential benefits they offer to society are immense. From improving healthcare diagnostics to enhancing transportation systems, AI has the power to revolutionize how we live and work. This rapid progress also raises ethical concerns regarding privacy, bias, and accountability. It is essential for developers, policymakers, and stakeholders to prioritize ethical considerations in the design and implementation of AI systems to ensure they align with societal values and norms. One of the key challenges in balancing innovation with ethical AI development lies in the need for clear regulations and guidelines to govern the deployment of these technologies. Developing a robust regulatory framework that addresses issues such as data privacy, algorithmic bias, and autonomous decision-making is crucial to building trust in AI systems. Promoting transparency and accountability in AI development processes can help mitigate potential risks and ensure that these technologies are used responsibly. By establishing clear ethical guidelines and standards, we can safeguard against the negative consequences of unchecked AI advancement and promote the responsible use of these powerful tools. Fostering a culture of ethical leadership and social responsibility within the AI community is essential to ensure that innovation is driven by ethical principles. Emphasizing the importance of diversity, inclusivity, and fairness in AI research and development can help prevent the perpetuation of biases and discriminatory practices in AI systems. By encouraging interdisciplinary collaboration and diverse perspectives, we can create AI technologies that are not only innovative but also ethically sound. By striking a balance between technological advancement and ethical considerations, we can harness the full potential of AI to benefit society while upholding our ethical responsibilities.

VII. TECHNOLOGICAL SINGULARITY PREDICTIONS

In considering the predictions surrounding the technological singularity, it is crucial to assess the potential benefits and risks that come with the advancement of AI. The exponential growth in AI capabilities has the capacity to revolutionize various industries, improving efficiency and productivity in ways previously unimaginable. In healthcare, AI-powered diagnostic tools can enhance the accuracy of disease detection, leading to earlier interventions and better patient outcomes. These advancements also raise concerns about data privacy, algorithm bias, and the displacement of human jobs. It is imperative to strike a balance between embracing AIs potential and mitigating its negative consequences through robust ethical guidelines and regulatory frameworks. The evolving landscape of AI technology underscores the importance of societys readiness to navigate the complexities that come with higher AI capabilities. One key aspect that requires attention is education and job training to equip individuals with the skills needed to work alongside AI systems. As automation becomes more prevalent, there is a growing need for a workforce that can adapt to new roles and collaborate effectively with AI technologies. The potential impact of AI on employment patterns and income inequality must be carefully considered to prevent widespread social upheaval. By investing in retraining programs and promoting lifelong learning initiatives, society can better prepare for the challenges posed by technological singularity predictions. In contemplating the implications of technological singularity predictions, it becomes evident that a proactive approach is essential to harness the benefits of AI while mitigating the associated risks. This calls for a concerted effort to establish clear guidelines for the ethical development and deployment of AI systems, ensuring transparency, accountability, and human-centric values are upheld. Fostering a culture of continuous learning and innovation will be crucial in enabling individuals and organizations to adapt to the rapidly changing landscape of AI technologies. The success of navigating the challenges posed by the technological singularity will hinge on our ability to foster a collaborative and responsible approach towards AI advancement, one that prioritizes the well-being of society as a whole.

Key proponents of the technological singularity theory

One key proponent of the technological singularity theory is Ray Kurzweil, a renowned futurist and author who predicts that AI will soon reach a level of intelligence superior to humans. Kurzweil argues that as AI continues to advance exponentially, it will eventually surpass human cognitive abilities, leading to a radical transformation of society. He believes that this moment of singularity will bring both unprecedented opportunities for progress and profound challenges for humanity to navigate. Kurzweils optimistic view of the singularity emphasizes the potential for AI to enhance human capabilities and solve complex problems, while also underscoring the need for careful planning to ensure that the transition is managed effectively. Another prominent figure in the discussion of the technological singularity is Nick Bostrom, a philosopher and professor at the University of Oxford. Bostroms work focuses on the ethical and existential implications of advanced artificial intelligence, exploring scenarios where AI could pose risks to humanity if not properly controlled. He raises concerns about the potential for superintelligent AI to act in ways that are harmful to human interests, highlighting the importance of developing robust ethical frameworks and control mechanisms to guide the development of AI. Bostroms critical perspective on the singularity emphasizes the need for proactive measures to address the challenges posed by increasingly intelligent machines. Elon Musk, the visionary founder of SpaceX and Tesla, is also a vocal advocate for addressing the risks associated with AI and the singularity. Musk has warned about the potential dangers of uncontrolled AI development, arguing that it could pose existential threats to humanity if not approached with caution. He advocates for proactive regulation and oversight of AI research and implementation to ensure that the technology is aligned with human values and interests. Musks stance on the singularity underscores the importance of integrating safety measures and ethical considerations into the development of advanced AI systems to prevent unintended consequences and safeguard the well-being of society.

Different scenarios of AI surpassing human intelligence

One potential scenario of AI surpassing human intelligence is the emergence of superintelligent machines capable of solving complex problems that are beyond human comprehension. These machines would possess an unprecedented level of cognitive abilities, enabling them to make decisions and develop strategies at a speed and accuracy far superior to human capabilities.

This scenario raises concerns about the implications of relying on machines that may operate beyond our control or understanding, leading to potential risks and uncertainties in various domains. The prospect of superintelligent AI highlights the need for robust safety measures and ethical guidelines to ensure that these systems align with human values and goals. Another scenario involves the integration of AI into every aspect of society, transforming the way we live and work on a fundamental level. As AI systems become increasingly sophisticated and autonomous, they could take over tasks traditionally performed by humans, leading to widespread automation and potentially displacing millions of jobs. This shift towards a more AI-driven society raises questions about the distribution of wealth, the redefinition of work and leisure, and the impact on individual well-being and identity. The potential economic and social ramifications of AI surpassing human intelligence underscore the importance of developing strategies to mitigate inequalities and ensure that the benefits of technological progress are shared equitably. A different perspective on AI surpassing human intelligence involves the potential for collaboration between humans and machines, leading to enhanced creativity, problem-solving, and innovation. Rather than viewing AI as a competitive force that threatens human dominance, this scenario envisions a symbiotic relationship where AI augments human capabilities and expands the possibilities for collective intelligence. By leveraging the strengths of both humans and machines, society could unlock new opportunities for scientific discovery, artistic expression, and societal advancement. This collaborative approach to AI surpassing human intelligence emphasizes the potential for mutual benefit and shared progress, highlighting the transformative power of combining human ingenuity with artificial intelligence.

Implications of reaching the technological singularity

As society approaches the technological singularity, one of the key implications that come to the forefront is the potential for massive disruption across various industries. The advancements in artificial intelligence, particularly in areas such as machine learning and neural networks, are poised to revolutionize how businesses operate. With AI capable of processing large amounts of data at unprecedented speeds, companies can streamline operations, improve efficiency, and enhance decision-making processes. This shift towards automation may also lead to job displacement as tasks once performed by humans are taken over by machines. This raises concerns about the future of work and the need for retraining programs to help individuals adapt to the changing landscape. Reaching the technological singularity also poses ethical challenges that must be addressed proactively. As AI systems become more sophisticated and autonomous, questions around accountability, bias, and privacy become increasingly pertinent. Ensuring that AI operates in a transparent and responsible manner requires the development of robust ethical frameworks and regulatory guidelines. It is essential for policymakers, technologists, and ethicists to collaborate in creating policies that safeguard against the potential misuse of AI and promote its beneficial applications. By fostering a culture of responsibility and accountability, we can mitigate the risks associated with advanced AI technologies and nurture trust among users and stakeholders. The impact of the technological singularity extends beyond economic and ethical considerations to encompass societal implications as well. As AI continues to evolve and infiltrate various aspects of our daily lives, it prompts a reevaluation of our understanding of intelligence and consciousness. The prospect of machines achieving human-like cognition raises profound philosophical questions about the nature of being and our place in the world. It challenges us to reconsider our relationships with technology and the boundaries between human and machine. By grappling with these existential questions, we can better prepare ourselves for a future where AI plays an increasingly influential role in shaping society.

VIII. SOCIETAL PREPAREDNESS FOR HIGHER AI

On the topic of societal preparedness for higher AI, it is essential to consider the implications of AI on various aspects of human life. One crucial aspect to focus on is the workforce and job market. As AI continues to advance and automate tasks traditionally done by humans, there is a looming concern about the potential displacement of workers. It is imperative for society to proactively address this issue by implementing training programs and reskilling initiatives to equip workers with the skills needed for the jobs of the future. By investing in education and providing support for those affected by automation, society can mitigate the negative impacts of AI on employment. The ethical considerations surrounding the development and deployment of higher AI must be carefully examined. As AI systems become more sophisticated and autonomous, there is a growing need for clear ethical guidelines to ensure that AI aligns with human values and interests. This includes ensuring transparency in AI decision-making processes and creating mechanisms for accountability in case of unintended consequences. By establishing ethical frameworks, society can navigate the complexities of AI technologies while upholding moral standards and protecting human rights. In addition to addressing workforce and ethical considerations, societal preparedness for higher AI also entails fostering a culture of collaboration between humans and machines. As AI technologies evolve, it is crucial for individuals to develop the skills and mindset necessary to work alongside intelligent machines effectively. This requires promoting interdisciplinary education that integrates AI concepts into various fields and encourages creative problem-solving and critical thinking. By cultivating a workforce that is adept at collaborating with AI, society can harness the full potential of these technologies while ensuring that human ingenuity remains at the forefront of innovation.

Education and upskilling for the AI era

In the era of AI, education and upskilling play a critical role in preparing society for the advancements and changes that come with higher AI. As automation becomes more prevalent across industries, there is a growing need for individuals with skills that complement AI systems. This includes not only technical proficiency in programming and data analysis but also soft skills such as creativity, adaptability, and emotional intelligence. Educational institutions must adapt their curricula to reflect these evolving needs, offering courses and programs that equip students with the tools to thrive in a digitally driven world. Ongoing upskilling and training opportunities for current professionals are essential to ensure that they can leverage AI technologies effectively in their respective fields. The pace at which AI technology is advancing requires a shift in the traditional approach to education. Continuous learning and upskilling are no longer optional but imperative to remain relevant in an AI-driven economy. Individuals must embrace a growth mindset, viewing education as a lifelong journey rather than a one-time event. This mindset fosters a culture of curiosity and innovation, driving individuals to continuously acquire new skills and knowledge. Institutions and organizations must also prioritize investing in employee development, offering training programs and resources to support their workforce in adapting to the changing technological landscape. By nurturing a culture of lifelong learning, society can cultivate a skilled workforce that is capable of embracing the opportunities and challenges presented by higher AI. In the face of the imminent technological singularity, education and upskilling serve as key pillars in ensuring a smooth transition into a future dominated by AI. By equipping individuals with the necessary skills and knowledge, society can harness the potential of AI to drive innovation and progress. This transformation must be accompanied by a commitment to ethical considerations and social responsibility. As AI continues to shape our world, it is essential that education not only focuses on technical expertise but also instills values such as empathy, ethics, and critical thinking. By fostering a holistic approach to education that integrates both technical skills and humanistic principles, society can navigate the complexities of the AI era with empathy, integrity, and foresight.

Social acceptance of AI technologies

As society continues to witness the rapid advancements in AI technologies, the question of social acceptance becomes increasingly relevant. The fear of the unknown often leads to skepticism and resistance towards AI, as people grapple with the idea of machines outperforming humans in various tasks. It is crucial to recognize that AI has the potential to revolutionize industries, improve efficiency, and enhance our quality of life. By fostering a deeper understanding of AI and its capabilities, society can embrace these technologies and harness their benefits effectively. One of the key factors that influence the social acceptance of AI is transparency in its development and deployment. The lack of clarity surrounding how AI systems operate and make decisions can lead to mistrust and apprehension among the general public. Establishing clear guidelines and regulations for the ethical use of AI is essential to build trust and ensure that these technologies are aligned with societal values and norms. By promoting transparency and accountability, stakeholders can work towards creating a more inclusive and supportive environment for the integration of AI into everyday life. Education plays a crucial role in shaping attitudes towards AI and fostering acceptance within society. By investing in programs that teach individuals about the potential of AI, its limitations, and ethical considerations, we can empower the workforce of the future to adapt and collaborate with these emerging technologies. Equipping people with the knowledge and skills to engage with AI in a meaningful way can bridge the gap between apprehension and acceptance, paving the way for a more harmonious coexistence between humans and machines. Social acceptance of AI technologies is contingent upon building trust, promoting transparency, and fostering a culture of education and collaboration within society.

Addressing biases and diversity in AI systems

In order to address biases and promote diversity in AI systems, it is crucial to first understand the underlying factors that contribute to these issues. One of the main challenges lies in the data used to train AI models, as biases present in the data can lead to biased outcomes. A machine learning algorithm trained on historical hiring data that favored a specific demographic may perpetuate discrimination in future hiring processes. It is essential to carefully curate and clean the training data to mitigate biases and ensure fair and accurate results. Diverse teams of developers and researchers can bring different perspectives and insights to the design and implementation of AI systems, helping to identify and rectify biases before they become ingrained in the technology. Transparency and accountability are key principles in addressing biases and promoting diversity in AI systems. Organizations developing AI technologies should be transparent about the methods and data used in their models, allowing for external scrutiny and auditability. By making the decision-making processes of AI systems more transparent, it becomes easier to identify and correct biases that may have been inadvertently incorporated. Accountability mechanisms, such as impact assessments and oversight committees, can also help ensure that AI systems are being used ethically and in accordance with legal and societal norms. Fostering a culture of transparency and accountability within the AI community can play a crucial role in building trust and mitigating biases in these technologies. Ongoing education and training programs are vital for addressing biases and promoting diversity in AI systems. By providing opportunities for individuals from diverse backgrounds to learn and work in the field of AI, we can cultivate a more inclusive and representative community of AI researchers and practitioners. These programs can help bridge the gap between underrepresented groups and the tech industry, fostering a more equitable distribution of skills and opportunities. Promoting ethical considerations and awareness of bias issues in AI education can empower future generations to develop technologies that are fair, inclusive, and socially responsible. By investing in education and training initiatives, we can proactively address biases and promote diversity in AI systems, laying the groundwork for a more equitable and inclusive future.

IX. FUTURE PROSPECTS OF AI DEVELOPMENT

As we consider the future prospects of AI development, one key aspect that emerges is the issue of control and governance. With advanced AI systems potentially surpassing human cognitive abilities, the need for robust ethical frameworks and regulations becomes paramount. Without clear guidelines and oversight, the risks associated with autonomous AI decision-making could lead to unintended consequences. Ensuring that AI remains aligned with human values and goals will be a significant challenge for policymakers and technologists alike. Establishing a framework that promotes responsible AI development and deployment is crucial to navigating the complexities of this technological landscape. Another critical consideration in the trajectory of AI advancement is the impact on the workforce and economy. As AI technologies become more sophisticated and capable of performing a wide range of tasks, there is a growing concern about the displacement of human labor. The potential for mass unemployment resulting from automation raises important questions about the future of work and the redistribution of societal resources. Addressing these challenges will require strategic planning and collaboration across multiple sectors to mitigate the negative consequences of AI on employment while harnessing its potential to create new opportunities and drive economic growth. The future of AI development presents both immense promise and significant challenges for society. While the technological advancements in AI hold the potential to revolutionize various industries and improve our quality of life, they also raise complex ethical, regulatory, and socioeconomic issues that must be addressed. As we stand on the brink of the technological singularity, it is essential to approach AI innovation with caution and foresight, ensuring that the benefits are equitably distributed and that humanity retains agency over the transformative powers of artificial intelligence. Only through thoughtful and collaborative efforts can we navigate the complexities of a future where AI plays an increasingly prominent role in shaping our world.

Potential breakthroughs in AI research

One promising area of research in AI revolves around the development of explainable AI, which aims to enhance transparency and interpretability in complex machine learning models. By providing insights into how AI systems reach decisions, researchers can improve trust in these technologies, paving the way for their broader adoption across various domains. Through methods like attention mechanisms and interpretability tools, explainable AI seeks to bridge the gap between AI capabilities and human comprehension, ensuring that algorithms are not perceived as black boxes but rather as tools that can be understood and validated by experts and non-experts alike. Another breakthrough in AI research lies in the realm of generative adversarial networks (GANs), a unique architecture that pits two neural networks against each other to generate authentic-looking data. From creating photorealistic images to composing music, GANs have showcased remarkable potential in creative fields, pushing the boundaries of what AI can achieve beyond traditional tasks. By enabling AI to produce original content and explore creative spaces, GANs open up new avenues for innovation and artistic expression, demonstrating the versatility and adaptability of AI in diverse contexts. The integration of AI with other emerging technologies like quantum computing holds immense promise for accelerating the pace of AI research and development. Quantum AI combines the power of quantum computings vast computational capabilities with AI algorithms to tackle complex problems more efficiently. By leveraging quantum properties such as superposition and entanglement, researchers can explore new frontiers in machine learning and optimization, driving advancements in AI capabilities that were previously unimaginable. This convergence of quantum technology and AI heralds a new era of innovation, with the potential to unlock unprecedented breakthroughs in scientific discovery and technological progress.

Integration of AI with other emerging technologies

The integration of AI with other emerging technologies such as blockchain and virtual reality has the potential to revolutionize various industries. By combining AI with blockchain, businesses can enhance security, transparency, and efficiency in their operations. Smart contracts powered by AI algorithms can streamline processes and reduce the need for intermediaries, increasing trust among parties. AI in virtual reality applications can provide personalized and immersive experiences, driving innovation in areas like gaming, training simulations, and virtual meetings. The synergy between these technologies opens up new possibilities for businesses to create unique solutions that cater to evolving customer needs while staying ahead of the competition. In the realm of healthcare, the fusion of AI with biotechnology is opening up unprecedented avenues for personalized medicine and disease diagnosis. AI-powered algorithms can analyze vast amounts of genomic data to identify patterns and predict individual responses to treatments. This has the potential to revolutionize the field by enabling tailored treatment plans that maximize efficacy and minimize side effects. The integration of AI with telemedicine technologies allows for remote consultations, real-time monitoring, and personalized health assessments. As these technologies evolve and converge, healthcare providers can offer more efficient and accessible care to patients, ultimately improving health outcomes and reducing healthcare costs. Looking ahead, the convergence of AI with the Internet of Things (IoT) holds immense promise for smart cities and connected ecosystems. By embedding AI algorithms into IoT devices, such as sensors and smart appliances, cities can optimize energy usage, traffic flow, and waste management systems. This interconnected network of devices can collect real-time data, analyze patterns, and make autonomous decisions to improve the quality of urban life. The integration of AI with IoT devices enables predictive maintenance, detecting issues before they escalate and reducing downtime. As these technologies merge, the potential for smart, sustainable, and efficient urban environments becomes increasingly tangible, paving the way for a more interconnected and intelligent future.

Long-term impact of AI on society and humanity

One of the overarching concerns surrounding the long-term impact of AI on society and humanity is the potential disruption it may cause in various sectors. As AI continues to advance, there is a growing fear that automation will lead to the replacement of human workers across industries. This could result in widespread job loss and economic instability, raising questions about how society will adapt to a future where robots and algorithms take on more tasks currently performed by humans. The implications for income inequality and social welfare programs are significant, warranting careful consideration and proactive measures to mitigate any negative effects. The integration of AI into everyday life raises ethical dilemmas that must be addressed to ensure the well-being and rights of individuals are protected. Issues such as data privacy, algorithmic bias, and the potential for misuse of AI technologies underscore the importance of establishing clear ethical guidelines and regulations. Without proper oversight, there is a risk that AI systems could perpetuate discrimination or infringe on personal liberties, highlighting the need for robust governance frameworks to safeguard against such outcomes. The ethical implications of AI extend beyond individual rights, also encompassing broader societal values and norms that must be upheld in the face of technological advancement. In addition to the immediate challenges posed by AI, there are also profound philosophical questions about the long-term implications for humanity as a whole. As AI systems become more sophisticated and autonomous, there is a looming possibility of a shift in power dynamics between humans and machines. The potential for AI to surpass human intelligence raises concerns about control, agency, and even the very nature of consciousness itself. Exploring these existential questions is essential in preparing for a future where AI may play an increasingly prominent role in shaping the course of society and humanity. As we venture further into the realm of higher AI, it is crucial to engage in thoughtful discourse and re-flection on the ultimate implications for the future of our species.

X. ETHICAL CONSIDERATIONS IN AI DEVELOPMENT

The development of AI raises profound ethical considerations that cannot be overlooked. As AI systems become more autonomous and capable of complex decision-making, questions of accountability and transparency come to the forefront. Ensuring that AI algorithms are fair, unbiased, and do not perpetuate harmful stereotypes is crucial in promoting ethical AI development. Issues related to data privacy and security must be carefully addressed to protect individuals personal information from misuse or exploitation. By establishing ethical guidelines and standards for AI development, society can mitigate the risks associated with AI technologies and promote their responsible use for the benefit of all. Ethical considerations in AI development also extend to the potential impact on society as a whole. The increasing deployment of AI systems in various industries may lead to job displacement and widening socioeconomic inequalities. It is essential to anticipate and address these challenges through thoughtful ethical frameworks that prioritize the well-being of individuals and communities. Ensuring that AI technologies are developed and used in a manner that respects human rights and dignity is essential in safeguarding against potential abuses of power and discrimination. By incorporating ethical considerations into AI development processes, we can strive to create a more just and equitable society that leverages AI for the common good. In light of the rapid advancements in AI technology, fostering a culture of ethical responsibility and accountability is imperative for navigating the complexities of higher AI. Educating the public about the ethical implications of AI and empowering individuals to participate in ethical decision-making processes are fundamental steps in creating a more inclusive and equitable AI ecosystem. Collaboration between interdisciplinary stakeholders, including technologists, policymakers, and ethicists, is essential for developing comprehensive ethical guidelines that reflect diverse perspectives and values. By proactively addressing ethical considerations in AI development, we can steer towards a future where AI serves as a force for positive social change, rather than exacerbating existing inequalities or perpetuating harm.

Bias and fairness in AI algorithms

One of the key concerns in the development and deployment of AI algorithms is the presence of bias, which can lead to unfair outcomes. Bias can creep into these algorithms through various means, such as biased training data or the design of the algorithm itself. If an AI system is trained on data that disproportionately represents one demographic group over another, it may make inaccurate or unfair decisions when applied in real-world scenarios. This bias can perpetuate and even exacerbate existing societal inequalities, posing a significant challenge to the goal of creating fair and equitable AI systems. Addressing bias in AI algorithms requires a multifaceted approach that involves careful data curation, algorithmic transparency, and ongoing evaluation of outcomes. By taking steps to actively mitigate bias in the development process, developers can work towards creating more fair and trustworthy AI systems. This may involve incorporating diverse perspectives in the design and testing phases, as well as implementing bias detection tools to monitor and correct for any unintended biases that arise. By fostering a culture of fairness and inclusivity in AI development, stakeholders can move towards a more ethical and responsible deployment of AI technologies. Ensuring fairness in AI algorithms is crucial not only for upholding ethical standards but also for building trust with users and stakeholders. Fairness promotes accountability and reliability in AI systems, which are essential for widespread adoption and acceptance. By prioritizing fairness and transparency in algorithm development, developers can help mitigate the risks of unintended consequences and discriminatory outcomes. The pursuit of fair AI algorithms is essential for realizing the full potential of AI in transforming industries and society as a whole.

Privacy concerns in AI data collection

Given the rapid advancements in AI technologies, privacy concerns surrounding AI data collection have become a significant issue in todays society. As AI systems become more integrated into various aspects of our lives, the amount of data being collected and analyzed is growing exponentially. This raises questions about who has access to this data, how it is being used, and the potential implications for individual privacy. Without proper safeguards in place, there is a risk that sensitive personal information could be misused or exploited for commercial gain without the consent of the individuals involved. One of the key concerns surrounding AI data collection is the lack of transparency in how data is being collected and used. Many AI algorithms rely on large datasets to train and improve their performance, often without clear information provided to individuals about what data is being collected, how it is being used, and who has access to it. This lack of transparency can lead to issues of consent and control over personal information, raising ethical questions about the trade-off between privacy and the benefits of AI technologies. As AI continues to evolve and become more ingrained in our daily lives, it is crucial that measures are put in place to ensure transparency and accountability in data collection practices. The potential for AI systems to infringe upon individual privacy rights is a pressing concern that must be addressed. With the ability to analyze vast amounts of data and make predictions about human behavior, AI technologies have the power to influence decisions that can have profound impacts on individuals lives. This raises important questions about data security, data ownership, and the potential for discrimination or bias in AI algorithms. To mitigate these risks, it is essential for policymakers, developers, and users to work together to establish clear guidelines and regulations that protect individual privacy while still fostering innovation in AI technology. By addressing these privacy concerns proactively, we can ensure that the benefits of AI can be realized while safeguarding the privacy rights of individuals.

Transparency and accountability in AI decision-making

In the rapidly evolving landscape of artificial intelligence, the issues of transparency and accountability in AI decision-making have become increasingly pertinent. As AI systems become more complex and autonomous, the need for clear understanding of how decisions are made and who is responsible for them is paramount. Without transparency, users and stakeholders are left in the dark about the reasoning behind AI decisions, leading to potential mistrust and ethical concerns. Without accountability mechanisms in place, there is a risk that AI systems may make biased or harmful decisions without any consequences for those responsible for their design and deployment. One approach to addressing the challenges of transparency and accountability in AI decision-making is through the implementation of explainable AI (XAI) systems. These systems are designed to provide human-readable explanations for the decisions made by AI algorithms, allowing users to understand the reasoning behind recommendations or actions taken. By making AI processes more transparent and interpretable, XAI can help build trust in AI technologies and enable effective oversight and accountability. Establishing clear guidelines and regulations for AI development and deployment can ensure that developers and organizations are held responsible for the decisions made by AI systems. As society moves towards a future where AI plays an increasingly central role in decision-making processes, ensuring transparency and accountability in AI decision-making is crucial. By embracing XAI and implementing robust regulatory frameworks, we can foster trust in AI technologies and mitigate potential risks associated with their use. Promoting transparency and accountability in AI decision-making will be essential in shaping a future where AI serves the common good and upholds ethical standards. As we stand on the brink of the technological singularity, it is imperative that we prioritize responsible AI development to navigate this transformative landscape successfully.

XI. AI GOVERNANCE AND REGULATION

AI governance and regulation play a crucial role in shaping the development and deployment of advanced technologies. As AI continues to evolve and demonstrate increasing capabilities, there is a growing recognition of the need to establish clear guidelines and frameworks to ensure its responsible use. Without proper governance, AI systems could pose significant risks in terms of privacy, security, and bias. By implementing regulations that promote transparency, accountability, and ethical standards, it is possible to harness the potential of AI while minimizing potential negative impacts. Regulations can help build trust among the public and mitigate concerns about the misuse of AI technologies. One key aspect of AI governance is the establishment of standards for data privacy and security. As AI systems rely on vast amounts of data to function effectively, there is a need to protect sensitive information from unauthorized access or misuse. By defining clear guidelines for data collection, storage, and usage, regulations can ensure that personal privacy is respected and that data is handled in a secure and responsible manner. Regulations can help address concerns about algorithmic bias and discrimination by requiring transparency in the development and deployment of AI systems. This can help prevent biased outcomes and promote fairness and equality in decision-making processes. In order to effectively govern AI technologies, it is essential to adopt a multi-stakeholder approach that involves collaboration between government agencies, industry stakeholders, and civil society organizations. By engaging a diverse range of perspectives and expertise, regulations can be designed to address the complex challenges posed by AI in a holistic and inclusive manner. Ongoing dialogue and cooperation among various stakeholders can facilitate the adaptation of regulations to the rapidly evolving technological landscape. In this way, AI governance and regulation can serve as a key tool in shaping the future of AI in a way that benefits society as a whole.

International standards for AI development

Another crucial aspect in the development of AI is the establishment of international standards. With AI becoming increasingly prevalent in various sectors worldwide, it is imperative to create a set of guidelines that ensure ethical practices and responsible deployment of these technologies. International standards would serve as a framework for developers and manufacturers to abide by, promoting transparency and accountability in AI systems. By having universally accepted regulations, countries can work together to address potential risks and ensure that AI is used for the betterment of society as a whole. International standards for AI development can help eliminate disparities between different regions in terms of regulatory practices. As AI becomes more integrated into global industries, having consistent guidelines can facilitate smoother collaboration and exchange of technology across borders. This harmonization of standards can also promote innovation by providing a level playing field for developers from different countries, leading to a more competitive and dynamic AI ecosystem. International standards can contribute to the growth and advancement of AI technology on a global scale, fostering a more cohesive and cooperative international community. International standards can play a pivotal role in addressing ethical considerations that arise with the advancement of artificial intelligence. By establishing guidelines for the ethical development and use of AI, countries can ensure that these technologies prioritize human well-being and respect fundamental rights. This ethical framework can help mitigate concerns related to privacy, bias, and discrimination in AI systems, fostering trust and acceptance among users and stakeholders. Through a concerted effort to uphold ethical standards, the international community can shape the future of AI development in a way that aligns with the values and expectations of society.

Legal frameworks for AI liability and accountability

Moving forward, the legal frameworks for AI liability and accountability are crucial aspects that must be carefully considered as we advance towards higher AI capabilities. The current legal landscape surrounding AI is complex and ambiguous, leading to challenges in determining responsibility in cases of AI malfunctions or errors. Establishing clear guidelines on who is liable when AI systems make critical decisions is essential to ensure accountability and protect individuals from potential harm. As AI technologies continue to evolve, it is imperative for regulators to adapt and develop comprehensive frameworks that address the unique challenges posed by autonomous systems. Addressing AI liability is not simply a matter of assigning blame, but also involves understanding the ethical implications of AI decision-making. The legal frameworks must be designed to uphold ethical standards and promote transparency in the development and deployment of AI systems. This requires a collaborative effort between policymakers, researchers, technology developers, and other stakeholders to establish a set of ethical principles that guide AI applications in a responsible manner. By incorporating ethical considerations into legal frameworks, we can create a more equitable and trustworthy environment for the integration of AI technologies into society. Navigating the complexities of AI liability and accountability requires a multi-dimensional approach that considers legal, ethical, and societal implications. As we stand on the brink of higher AI capabilities, it is essential to proactively address these challenges to ensure that AI systems align with human values and priorities. By fostering collaboration between experts across various fields and developing adaptive legal frameworks, we can pave the way for a future where AI technologies enhance human capabilities while upholding ethical standards and accountability. Only through careful consideration and proactive measures can we harness the full potential of AI for the betterment of society.

Oversight mechanisms for AI deployment

Despite the potential benefits of AI deployment, concerns have been raised about the lack of sufficient oversight mechanisms to regulate its use. One key aspect of oversight is the establishment of clear ethical guidelines to govern the development and deployment of AI technologies. These guidelines can help ensure that AI systems are designed and used in a way that aligns with societal values and respects fundamental human rights. By creating a framework of ethical principles, policymakers can help promote transparency, accountability, and fairness in AI applications. Oversight mechanisms should include robust regulatory frameworks that govern the testing, validation, and deployment of AI systems across various sectors. These regulations can help mitigate risks associated with AI technologies, such as bias, discrimination, and privacy violations. By implementing standards and guidelines for AI development, governments can create a level playing field for companies and researchers while safeguarding the interests of users and the general public. Regulatory oversight can help address potential ethical dilemmas and ensure that AI is used responsibly and ethically. In addition to ethical principles and regulatory frameworks, oversight mechanisms for AI deployment should also include mechanisms for ongoing monitoring, evaluation, and auditing of AI systems in real-world settings. This can help identify and address potential issues or unintended consequences that may arise from the use of AI technologies. By conducting regular audits and reviews of AI systems, stakeholders can ensure that these technologies are being used in a safe, transparent, and accountable manner. Comprehensive oversight mechanisms are essential to ensure the responsible and ethical deployment of AI in society.

XII. AI IN CREATIVE INDUSTRIES

Another industry that has been greatly impacted by the rise of AI is the creative sector. AI is revolutionizing the way creative content is produced, from generating music and writing articles to designing visual art. Machine learning algorithms are being used to analyze patterns in existing works and create new pieces with minimal human intervention. This has led to a democratization of creativity, allowing individuals with no formal training to access tools that can assist them in producing high-quality content. This also raises concerns about the originality of AI-generated works and the role of human artists in a world dominated by machine-generated art. AI has the potential to enhance the creative process by providing artists with new tools and resources to explore their creativity. AI algorithms can analyze large datasets of music, literature, and visual art to identify trends and patterns that can inspire new works. This can be particularly useful for artists seeking inspiration or struggling with creative blocks. AI can automate repetitive tasks, allowing artists to focus on more complex aspects of their work. There are valid concerns about the impact of AI on the authenticity and originality of artistic expression. Can a work created by a machine truly evoke the same emotional response as one created by a human artist? These questions highlight the ethical dilemmas and philosophical implications of integrating AI into the creative process. Despite the potential benefits of AI in the creative industries, there are also significant risks and challenges that need to be addressed. One major concern is the potential loss of artistic diversity and cultural richness if AI algorithms start to dictate trends and styles in creative content.

There are unresolved issues around copyright and ownership of AI-generated works, raising questions about who should be credited as the creator of such content. As AI continues to advance, it is crucial for policymakers, artists, and technologists to work together to establish clear guidelines and ethical frameworks to govern the use of AI in creative industries, ensuring that human creativity remains at the forefront of artistic expression.

AI-generated art and music

AI-generated art and music are burgeoning fields that showcase the creative potential of artificial intelligence. Through complex algorithms and data analysis, AI systems can now produce visual artworks and musical compositions that mimic human creativity. This has sparked a debate on the nature of art and the role of the artist in a world where machines can generate original pieces. While some argue that AI-generated art lacks the emotional depth and intentionality of human creations, others see it as a new form of artistic expression that pushes the boundaries of traditional art forms. The ability of AI to create art and music raises questions about the nature of creativity and the essence of what it means to be human. Can a machine truly replicate the complex emotions and experiences that inspire artists to create? While AI-generated pieces may lack the personal touch and unique perspective of a human artist, they offer a new lens through which to explore the creative process. By learning from vast databases of existing works, AI systems can generate innovative and unexpected compositions that challenge our preconceptions of what art and music can be. As AI continues to advance, the line between human and machine creativity may become increasingly blurred. The collaboration between artists and AI systems could lead to groundbreaking innovations in the arts, pushing the boundaries of what is possible. By harnessing the computational power of AI to augment human creativity, we may witness a renaissance in art and music that transcends traditional limitations. The emergence of AI-generated art and music invites us to ponder the true nature of creativity and the endless possibilities that arise from the intersection of technology and imagination.

Impact of AI on content creation

In the realm of content creation, AI is revolutionizing the way we generate and consume information. AI-powered tools, such as natural language processing algorithms and advanced data analytics, are enabling content creators to streamline their processes and produce high-quality materials more efficiently. AI can analyze user data to tailor content to specific audiences, improving engagement and driving conversions. By harnessing the power of AI, content creators can stay ahead of trends, predict user preferences, and deliver personalized experiences that resonate with consumers on a deeper level. AI has the potential to enhance creativity in content creation by offering innovative solutions and generating fresh ideas. Through machine learning algorithms, AI can sift through vast amounts of data to identify patterns and insights that humans may overlook. AI can assist in the creative process by providing suggestions for content structure, tone, and style, helping content creators refine their work and reach a broader audience. By collaborating with AI, content creators can explore new avenues, experiment with different formats, and push the boundaries of storytelling in ways that were previously unimaginable. While AI brings unprecedented opportunities to content creation, it also raises concerns about authenticity and accountability. As AI tools become more sophisticated, there is a risk that content creators may rely too heavily on automated solutions, compromising the integrity and originality of their work. There are ethical implications surrounding the use of AI in content creation, such as ensuring transparency in AI-generated content to avoid misinformation and manipulation. As we navigate the evolving landscape of AI in content creation, it is essential to strike a balance between leveraging technology to enhance creativity and upholding ethical standards to maintain trust and credibility with audiences.

Copyright and intellectual property issues in AI-generated works

In the realm of AI-generated works, copyright and intellectual property issues present complex challenges that require careful consideration. As AI systems become more advanced and capable of producing creative content, questions arise about who should hold the rights to these works. Unlike human creators, AI cannot be considered an author in the traditional sense, leading to ambiguity in assigning ownership. Legal frameworks will need to adapt to address this gap, determining whether ownership lies with the programmers, the users, or the AI itself. Clarifying these issues is essential to protect the interests of creators, encourage innovation, and prevent disputes over ownership rights. The emergence of AI-generated works blurs the line between originality and automation, raising concerns about plagiarism and the potential for widespread unauthorized use of content. Without clear guidelines on how to attribute authorship in AI-generated works, there is a risk of devaluing the creative contributions of human creators and undermining the integrity of intellectual property rights. Establishing robust mechanisms for identifying and protecting AI-generated content is crucial to maintain the credibility and integrity of the creative industries. By ensuring proper attribution and recognition for both human and AI contributions, the intellectual property landscape can evolve to accommodate the complexities of modern technology. The rapid pace of technological advancement in AI poses challenges for existing copyright laws and enforcement mechanisms. As AI continues to evolve and generate increasingly sophisticated works, traditional concepts of originality and authorship may need to be redefined to reflect the collaborative nature of human-AI interactions. In this evolving landscape, it is imperative for policymakers, legal experts, and industry stakeholders to engage in proactive dialogue and develop flexible frameworks that balance the interests of all parties involved. By fostering a harmonious relationship between creativity, innovation, and legal protections, society can navigate the complexities of AI-generated works while upholding the principles of intellectual property rights.

XIII. AI IN ENVIRONMENTAL SUSTAINABILITY

In the realm of environmental sustainability, AI holds great promise for addressing pressing ecological challenges. AI technologies can analyze vast amounts of data to optimize resource management, enhance energy efficiency, and minimize waste. AI-powered sensors and algorithms can monitor ecosystems in real-time, offering valuable insights into biodiversity conservation and climate change mitigation. By harnessing AIs predictive capabilities, organizations can develop more effective strategies for sustainable development, leading to improved environmental outcomes. AI plays a crucial role in revolutionizing renewable energy production and distribution. From optimizing solar panel placements to predicting wind patterns for more efficient energy generation, AI offers innovative solutions for transitioning towards a greener economy. By integrating AI into smart grids, energy systems can be optimized to reduce carbon emissions and enhance overall efficiency. These advancements pave the way for a more sustainable future, where renewable energy sources can meet increasing global demand while minimizing environmental impact. AI can aid in monitoring and managing natural disasters, such as hurricanes, wildfires, and floods, by analyzing patterns and predicting potential risks. Through AI-driven models, emergency response teams can better prepare for and respond to environmental crises, potentially saving lives and reducing damage to ecosystems. By utilizing AI technologies in disaster management, society can build resilience in the face of climate change-related events, ultimately contributing to a more sustainable and secure future for generations to come.

Applications of AI in climate change research

In the realm of climate change research, the applications of AI are proving to be invaluable in understanding and mitigating the effects of global warming. One key area where AI is making a significant impact is in climate modeling. By processing vast amounts of data from satellites, sensors, and climate models, AI algorithms can generate more accurate predictions of future climate patterns. This capability allows scientists to better anticipate extreme weather events, sea-level rise, and other consequences of climate change, leading to more effective strategies for adaptation and resilience. AI is being used to analyze climate data in ways that were previously impossible. Machine learning algorithms can detect subtle patterns and trends in large datasets, uncovering correlations and insights that human researchers might overlook. This enhanced data analysis is essential for identifying the root causes of climate change, assessing the effectiveness of mitigation measures, and developing innovative solutions to complex environmental challenges. By harnessing the power of AI, researchers can accelerate the pace of scientific discovery and drive more informed decision-making in the fight against climate change. AI technologies are facilitating the monitoring and surveillance of environmental changes on a global scale. From tracking deforestation in the Amazon rainforest to monitoring carbon emissions from industrial sources, AI-driven systems are enabling more efficient and accurate monitoring of key environmental indicators. This real-time monitoring capability allows policymakers to respond more swiftly to emerging threats to the environment, enabling a more proactive approach to conservation and sustainable management practices. By leveraging AI tools in climate change research, we can enhance our understanding of environmental processes, improve the precision of climate models, and ultimately work towards a more sustainable future for our planet.

AI solutions for sustainable resource management

AI solutions for sustainable resource management can revolutionize how we approach environmental challenges. By utilizing AI algorithms to analyze data, optimize processes, and predict future trends, organizations can make more informed decisions that lead to better resource management. AI can be applied to energy systems to increase efficiency, reduce waste, and promote renewable sources. By automating tasks that would be time-consuming and prone to human error, AI can help streamline operations and minimize environmental impact. This approach can not only benefit businesses by reducing costs but also contribute to a more sustainable future for our planet. AI can be instrumental in monitoring and managing natural resources such as water, forests, and wildlife. Through remote sensing technologies and data analysis, AI can provide real-time information on ecosystems, enabling proactive conservation efforts and early intervention in case of threats. By incorporating AI into resource management strategies, governments and conservation organizations can enhance their ability to protect biodiversity, mitigate climate change effects, and promote sustainable practices. This proactive approach can lead to more effective resource allocation, ensuring the long-term health of our ecosystems and the well-being of future generations. In addition to environmental applications, AI can also play a crucial role in optimizing supply chains and reducing waste in various industries. By utilizing predictive analytics and machine learning algorithms, companies can anticipate demand, optimize production schedules, and minimize inventory levels. This not only improves efficiency and reduces costs but also has a positive impact on the environment by lowering carbon emissions and resource consumption. AI-driven solutions for supply chain management can promote circular economy principles, encouraging the reuse and recycling of materials to create a more sustainable and efficient system. AI has the potential to revolutionize how we manage resources, promoting sustainability and responsible stewardship of our planet.

Ethical considerations in using AI for environmental conservation

In the realm of environmental conservation, ethical considerations play a crucial role in the integration of AI technologies. When utilizing AI for conservation purposes, it is essential to ensure that the data being collected and analyzed is done so in an ethical manner. This includes respecting the privacy and rights of individuals whose information may be involved in the process. There is a need to consider how AI algorithms are being trained and whether biases are being inadvertently incorporated into the systems. Ethical guidelines must be established to govern the use of AI in conservation efforts, preventing any negative impact on the environment or local communities. Transparency in the decision-making process is essential when employing AI for environmental conservation. The algorithms used in AI systems must be open and understandable, allowing for scrutiny and accountability. This transparency helps to build trust among stakeholders and ensures that the outcomes of AI applications are fair and unbiased. Engaging with local communities and incorporating their input into the development and implementation of AI technologies can lead to more effective and sustainable conservation practices. By involving diverse perspectives, the potential risks and benefits of using AI in conservation can be more thoroughly evaluated and addressed. In shaping the future of AI in environmental conservation, an interdisciplinary approach is key to navigating ethical challenges and ensuring responsible use of technology. Collaboration between conservationists, technologists, policymakers, and ethicists is crucial in developing frameworks that prioritize the well-being of ecosystems and communities. By fostering a dialogue between these diverse stakeholders, we can work towards harnessing the power of AI to drive positive change in conservation efforts while upholding ethical standards. By integrating ethical considerations into the deployment of AI technologies, we can strive for a harmonious coexistence between AI and the natural world.

XIV. AI IN GOVERNANCE AND PUBLIC POLICY

The integration of AI in governance and public policy is reshaping traditional models of decision-making and resource allocation. Governments are increasingly turning to AI systems to analyze vast amounts of data and predict trends that can inform policy development. By leveraging machine learning algorithms, policymakers can make more informed and data-driven decisions, leading to enhanced efficiency and effectiveness in public services. AI can be used to optimize transportation systems, healthcare delivery, and emergency response protocols, ultimately improving the quality of life for citizens. AI has the potential to increase transparency and accountability in governance by providing real-time insights into the impact of policies and programs. Through advanced analytics, governments can track the outcomes of their initiatives and adjust strategies accordingly to achieve better results. This data-driven approach can also help identify and address disparities in service delivery, ensuring that resources are allocated equitably. By harnessing the power of AI, governments can better respond to the needs of their constituents and foster a more inclusive and responsive public sector. The adoption of AI in governance raises important ethical and regulatory considerations that must be carefully addressed. As AI systems become more autonomous and decision-making processes are delegated to algorithms, questions arise regarding accountability, bias, and privacy protection. It is crucial for policymakers to establish clear guidelines and safeguards to ensure that AI technologies are deployed in a responsible and transparent manner. By fostering collaboration between policymakers, technologists, and ethicists, governments can harness the full potential of AI while mitigating the risks associated with its implementation in public policy.

AI in decision-making processes

One concern surrounding the integration of AI into decision-making processes is the potential for bias. Machine learning algorithms, when trained on biased data, can perpetuate and even exacerbate existing societal inequalities. In hiring processes, AI may inadvertently discriminate against certain demographics based on past patterns in the data it has been fed. This raises ethical concerns about the fairness and transparency of AI-driven decisions. Without proper oversight and regulation, AI systems could inadvertently reinforce harmful biases, leading to unintended consequences for individuals and society as a whole. The reliance on AI in decision-making processes begs the question of accountability. When a machine makes a decision, who is ultimately responsible for the outcome? In cases of error or harm caused by AI-driven decisions, pinpointing accountability becomes a complex issue. This lack of clarity raises concerns about the ethical implications of delegating crucial decisions to machines. As AI becomes more integrated into various aspects of society, establishing clear lines of responsibility and accountability will be essential to ensure the ethical and legal implications of AI-driven decisions are properly addressed. In light of these challenges, it is crucial to consider the role of human oversight in AI decision-making processes. While AI systems can process vast amounts of data at incredible speeds, human judgment and moral reasoning are still essential components of effective decision-making. Integrating human oversight into AI systems can help mitigate the risks of bias, enhance transparency, and ensure that ethical considerations are taken into account. By fostering collaboration between AI technologies and human intelligence, it is possible to harness the benefits of AI while upholding ethical standards and promoting responsible decision-making in an increasingly automated world.

Ethical implications of AI in public administration

The ethical implications of AI in public administration are significant due to the potential impact on governance, decision-making processes, and accountability. As AI systems are integrated into government agencies to streamline operations and improve efficiency, questions arise regarding the transparency and fairness of these systems. There is a concern that AI algorithms may inadvertently perpetuate biases or discrimination, leading to unjust outcomes in public policy. The use of AI in public administration raises concerns about data privacy and security, as sensitive information gathered by these systems could be at risk of misuse or unauthorized access. The implementation of AI in public administration also poses challenges in terms of accountability and responsibility. Who would be held accountable if an AI system makes a decision that harms individuals or communities? The lack of a clear framework for assigning responsibility in AI-driven decision-making processes raises issues of legal and ethical accountability. The potential for AI to outperform human decision-makers in certain tasks may diminish the role of public officials, leading to concerns about the delegation of power to non-human entities. These ethical dilemmas highlight the need for robust governance structures and ethical guidelines to ensure that AI in public administration aligns with democratic principles and values. Navigating the ethical implications of AI in public administration requires a delicate balance between technological advancement and ethical considerations. As AI continues to permeate government systems and processes, it is essential to prioritize transparency, accountability, and fairness in the deployment of these technologies. By developing clear guidelines for the ethical use of AI in public administration, policymakers can mitigate potential risks and promote the responsible adoption of AI for the benefit of society as a whole. Addressing the ethical challenges of AI in public administration requires a collaborative effort between government officials, technologists, ethicists, and the public to ensure that these technologies serve the common good.

Citizen engagement and transparency in AI-driven governance

In the realm of AI-driven governance, citizen engagement and transparency play crucial roles in ensuring accountability and ethical decision-making. As AI becomes increasingly integrated into governmental processes, it is essential for citizens to have a clear understanding of how these technologies are being utilized and how they may impact their lives. By fostering open communication channels between government entities, AI developers, and the public, transparency can help build trust and ensure that the algorithms driving governance are fair and unbiased. Citizen engagement in the design and implementation of AI systems can help address concerns about privacy, bias, and unintended consequences, ultimately leading to more inclusive and responsive governance. One of the key challenges in AI-driven governance is the potential for decision-making processes to become opaque and inaccessible to the average citizen. Without transparency, there is a risk that AI-driven systems may perpetuate or even exacerbate existing inequalities and biases, leading to unintended consequences for marginalized communities. To address this challenge, governments must prioritize transparency measures such as explainable AI, algorithmic audits, and public consultations to ensure that the decision-making processes behind AI technologies are comprehensible and accountable. By engaging citizens in discussions around the ethical implications of AI-driven governance, governments can work towards building a more just and equitable society. In the quest for effective citizen engagement and transparency in AI-driven governance, collaboration between policymakers, technologists, and civil society is essential. By creating multi-stakeholder forums where different perspectives can be heard and debated, decision-makers can develop policies that reflect a wide range of concerns and considerations. Public education campaigns can help increase awareness about the capabilities and limitations of AI technologies, empowering citizens to participate meaningfully in discussions about their use in governance. By prioritizing citizen engagement and transparency in AI-driven governance, societies can harness the potential of AI while upholding democratic values and ensuring that the benefits of these technologies are equitably distributed.

XV. AI AND HUMAN RIGHTS

In the realm of artificial intelligence, concerns about human rights have become increasingly prevalent as technology continues to advance at a rapid pace. One key issue is the potential for AI systems to infringe upon privacy rights, as data collection becomes more pervasive and sophisticated. Facial recognition technologies can track individuals movements without their consent, raising questions about surveillance and personal freedom. The use of AI in decision-making processes, such as in the criminal justice system or hiring practices, has sparked debates about bias and discrimination. These concerns highlight the need for clear guidelines and regulations to protect individuals rights in the age of AI. The intersection of AI and human rights extends to issues of transparency and accountability. As AI algorithms become more complex and opaque, it can be challenging to understand how decisions are made and to hold responsible parties accountable for their outcomes. In cases of algorithmic bias or errors, it may be difficult to identify the root causes and rectify the situation. This lack of transparency can undermine trust in AI systems and raise concerns about fairness and justice. There is a critical need for transparency requirements and mechanisms for auditing and oversight to ensure that AI systems operate ethically and responsibly. The use of AI in surveillance and social control raises profound ethical questions about autonomy and freedom of expression. In authoritarian regimes, AI-powered technologies are employed to monitor and suppress dissent, leading to widespread censorship and human rights violations. In democratic societies, similar concerns arise over the potential for AI to manipulate public discourse and infringe upon civil liberties. To address these challenges, a robust framework of human rights principles and guidelines must be established to guide the development and deployment of AI technologies. By upholding fundamental rights and values, society can ensure that AI serves humanity in a manner that is ethical, just, and conducive to the common good.

AI in surveillance and privacy rights

The integration of AI in surveillance systems raises concerns regarding privacy rights. The widespread use of AI-powered facial recognition technology, for instance, has sparked debates over the balance between security measures and individual liberties. Critics argue that constant monitoring by AI systems infringes on citizens rights to privacy and can lead to unwarranted surveillance and profiling. As AI algorithms become increasingly sophisticated in identifying and tracking individuals, the potential for abuse and misuse of personal data becomes more pronounced. This highlights the urgent need for robust regulations and ethical guidelines to govern the deployment of AI in surveillance to safeguard privacy rights. The advancement of AI in surveillance not only poses a threat to individual privacy but also challenges the notion of autonomy and freedom in society. The continuous monitoring and analysis of behavior through AI systems can have a chilling effect on individuals freedom of expression and movement. The pervasive nature of AI surveillance raises concerns about the erosion of civil liberties and the emergence of a surveillance state where citizens are constantly under scrutiny. The power dynamics between individuals and authorities are reshaped by the omnipresence of AI technologies, raising questions about the implications for democracy and human rights in a world increasingly reliant on surveillance technologies. In order to address the ethical and legal implications of AI in surveillance, policymakers and stakeholders must engage in a dialogue to establish clear guidelines and boundaries for the use of these technologies. It is essential to strike a balance between security concerns and the protection of fundamental rights, ensuring that the deployment of AI in surveillance is conducted transparently and accountably. By fostering collaboration between technology developers, policymakers, and civil society, it is possible to harness the benefits of AI while upholding privacy rights and preserving the autonomy of individuals in a digital age. Only through a concerted effort to regulate and monitor the use of AI in surveillance can we navigate the challenges posed by these technologies and safeguard the principles of a democratic society.

Bias and discrimination in AI systems

One of the critical concerns surrounding the advancement of AI is the issue of bias and discrimination within AI systems. While these technologies hold great potential for improving efficiency and decision-making in various fields, they are not immune to inheriting human biases. Machine learning algorithms trained on biased data may perpetuate discriminatory practices, such as racial profiling in criminal justice systems or gender bias in hiring processes. This raises serious ethical implications that must be addressed to ensure that AI systems do not perpetuate social inequalities. The opacity of AI algorithms poses a challenge in identifying and rectifying biases present in these systems. The complex and often black-box nature of deep learning models makes it difficult to understand how decisions are reached, leaving room for bias to go undetected. This lack of transparency not only undermines trust in AI technologies but also hinders efforts to hold developers and organizations accountable for discriminatory outcomes. As AI becomes increasingly integrated into society, it is crucial to prioritize transparency and accountability in the design and implementation of these systems to mitigate the risks of bias and discrimination. In light of these challenges, there is a pressing need for the establishment of ethical guidelines and regulatory frameworks to govern the development and deployment of AI technologies. These frameworks should address issues of bias and discrimination, emphasizing the importance of fairness, equity, and accountability in AI systems. By setting clear standards and guidelines for developers and organizations, regulators can promote ethical practices and ensure that AI systems are used responsibly and in a manner that respects human rights and diversity. Addressing bias and discrimination in AI is essential for building a future in which these technologies can benefit society as a whole.

Ensuring AI respects fundamental human rights

In the quest to ensure that AI respects fundamental human rights, it is essential to establish clear ethical guidelines and regulatory frameworks. These frameworks should address issues such as bias in AI algorithms, data privacy, and accountability in decision-making processes. By setting these standards, we can safeguard against potential harms and violations of human rights that may arise as AI systems become more advanced and pervasive in society. Implementing transparency measures can help increase trust in AI technologies, fostering a more harmonious relationship between humans and machines. One key aspect of ensuring AI respects fundamental human rights is promoting diversity and inclusion in the development and deployment of these technologies. By embracing a diverse range of perspectives and voices in the AI industry, we can avoid perpetuating biases and discrimination in AI systems. Involving stakeholders from different backgrounds can help surface ethical considerations that may not have been apparent otherwise. Through collaboration and cooperation, we can work towards creating AI systems that uphold human rights and promote equality and fairness for all members of society. In addition to ethical guidelines and diversity in AI development, it is crucial to empower individuals with knowledge and awareness of AI technologies and their implications for human rights. Education plays a key role in preparing people to engage with AI in a responsible and informed manner. By equipping individuals with the necessary skills to critically analyze AI systems and advocate for their rights, we can create a more inclusive and equitable society in which technology serves as a tool for positive change rather than a source of harm. A multi-faceted approach is necessary to ensure that AI respects fundamental human rights, encompassing ethical standards, diversity in development, and education for empowerment.

XVI. AI AND GLOBAL SECURITY

In the realm of global security, the integration of advanced AI systems presents both unprecedented opportunities and significant challenges. On the one hand, AI technologies have the potential to revolutionize military capabilities, enhancing strategic decision-making, precision targeting, and even autonomous weapon systems. This same potential raises concerns about the ethical implications of delegating life-and-death decisions to machines, as well as the risk of unintended consequences in conflict situations. The rapid evolution of AI raises urgent questions about the implications for traditional security paradigms and the need for international cooperation to establish norms and regulations. The proliferation of AI in various domains, including cybersecurity, surveillance, and information warfare, has created new vulnerabilities that can be exploited by malicious actors. As AI becomes increasingly sophisticated, the risk of cyberattacks and other forms of AI-driven threats grows, posing a significant challenge to global security. The interconnected nature of todays digital infrastructure means that a single AI-powered attack could have far-reaching implications, underscoring the need for robust defense mechanisms and cross-border collaboration to address emerging threats effectively. In light of these complex dynamics, policymakers and security experts must grapple with the dual imperative of harnessing the transformative potential of AI for security while mitigating the associated risks. This requires a holistic approach that combines technological innovation with ethical considerations, regulatory frameworks, and international cooperation. By fostering a multidisciplinary dialogue that engages stakeholders from government, industry, academia, and civil society, it becomes possible to navigate the intricacies of AI and global security and shape a future in which AI serves as a force for peace and stability rather than a source of conflict and instability.

AI in defense and military applications

AI has increasingly gained ground in defense and military applications, offering a wide range of potential benefits. One key advantage of AI in this context is its ability to gather and analyze massive amounts of data quickly and accurately, enabling military personnel to make more informed decisions in real-time. AI-powered drones can be used for surveillance missions, identifying potential threats and targets with high precision. This enhanced situational awareness can greatly improve the effectiveness of military operations while reducing risks to soldiers on the ground. AI can also be utilized for autonomous weapons systems, including unmanned aerial vehicles and ground-based robots. These systems have the potential to carry out tasks that are too dangerous or difficult for human soldiers, such as clearing minefields or conducting covert reconnaissance missions. While the use of autonomous weapons raises ethical concerns, proponents argue that they can help minimize collateral damage and civilian casualties in conflict zones. It is essential to establish clear guidelines and regulations to ensure that AI is used responsibly and in accordance with international humanitarian law. In addition to its operational benefits, AI in defense and military applications also presents new challenges and risks that must be carefully managed. Cybersecurity threats, for instance, can exploit vulnerabilities in AI systems to disrupt military operations or steal classified information. Ensuring the robustness and reliability of AI technologies in the face of evolving cyber threats will be critical for national security. The use of AI in warfare raises complex legal and ethical dilemmas, including questions about accountability and the potential for autonomous systems to make life-and-death decisions. As AI continues to advance, policymakers, military leaders, and ethicists must work together to address these challenges and ensure that AI is deployed in a manner that upholds human values and protects global security.

Cybersecurity challenges in the age of AI

In the age of AI, cybersecurity faces unprecedented challenges due to the complexity and sophistication of AI systems. One of the main concerns is the potential for AI-powered cyberattacks to be more targeted, stealthy, and difficult to detect than traditional methods. Machine learning algorithms can adapt and learn from new data, allowing cybercriminals to constantly evolve their tactics to bypass security measures. This dynamic threat landscape requires a proactive approach to cybersecurity, with a focus on continuous monitoring, threat intelligence, and rapid response capabilities. The use of AI in cybersecurity itself poses risks, as malicious actors can exploit vulnerabilities in AI systems to manipulate them for their advantage. Adversarial attacks, where subtle changes to input data can deceive AI algorithms, raise concerns about the reliability and trustworthiness of automated defense mechanisms. To address these challenges, cybersecurity professionals must not only understand the technical aspects of AI but also anticipate the ethical implications of its deployment. Ensuring the integrity and resilience of AI systems requires robust safeguards, transparent algorithms, and adherence to ethical standards to mitigate the potential for exploitation. As AI continues to advance, the interconnected nature of digital systems and critical infrastructure increases the potential impact of cyber threats on society. The convergence of AI with other emerging technologies, such as the Internet of Things and autonomous vehicles, amplifies the complexity and scale of cybersecurity challenges. This interconnected ecosystem requires holistic risk management strategies that encompass not only technological aspects but also regulatory frameworks, international cooperation, and public awareness. Strengthening cybersecurity resilience in the age of AI demands collaborative efforts between governments, industry stakeholders, and academia to navigate the evolving threat landscape and safeguard the future of digital innovation.

International cooperation in regulating AI weapons

In the context of the rapidly advancing field of artificial intelligence, the need for international cooperation in regulating AI weapons becomes increasingly urgent. As AI technologies continue to evolve and become more sophisticated, the potential for these tools to be used in warfare raises significant ethical and security concerns. Without a global framework in place to govern the development and deployment of AI weapons, there is a risk of destabilizing the international security landscape. International cooperation is essential to establish standards and norms that can guide the responsible use of AI in military contexts, ensuring that these technologies are employed in ways that comply with international law and respect human rights. Collaboration among nations in regulating AI weapons can help to mitigate the risks associated with unintended consequences and the potential for escalation in conflicts. By fostering dialogue and cooperation on AI governance, countries can work together to address common challenges and promote transparency in the development and deployment of AI technologies. This collective effort can also help to build trust among nations and reduce the likelihood of arms races driven by the pursuit of AI supremacy in military settings. International cooperation in regulating AI weapons is crucial for promoting peace and security in an increasingly interconnected world. By establishing clear rules and guidelines for the responsible use of AI technologies in warfare, countries can work together to prevent the misuse of these powerful tools and uphold ethical standards in military operations. Through ongoing collaboration and dialogue, the international community can navigate the complex challenges posed by AI weapons and ensure that these technologies are harnessed for the collective benefit of humanity.

XVII. AI AND EMOTIONAL INTELLIGENCE

The integration of emotional intelligence into AI systems is becoming increasingly relevant as technology progresses. Emotional intelligence involves the ability to perceive, understand, and manage emotions, both in oneself and in others. By incorporating emotional intelligence into AI, machines can better interact with humans, understand their emotions and respond appropriately. This can lead to more personalized and empathetic interactions, enhancing the overall user experience. The development of AI with emotional intelligence raises ethical considerations regarding the potential manipulation of human emotions. With machines becoming more capable of understanding and responding to emotions, there is a concern about how this knowledge could be used to influence individuals feelings and behavior. This highlights the importance of establishing guidelines and regulations to ensure that AI with emotional intelligence is used ethically and responsibly, safeguarding user privacy and autonomy. The intersection of AI and emotional intelligence represents a significant advancement in technology with the potential to revolutionize human-machine interactions. As this technology evolves, it is crucial to address ethical considerations and establish clear boundaries to prevent misuse. By incorporating emotional intelligence into AI systems thoughtfully and ethically, we can harness the benefits of enhanced interactions while mitigating the risks associated with the manipulation of human emotions. The development of AI with emotional intelligence requires a thoughtful and balanced approach to ensure that it serves the best interests of society as a whole.

Development of emotionally intelligent AI

In the pursuit of developing emotionally intelligent AI, researchers are incorporating advances in cognitive science and psychology to enable machines to recognize and respond to human emotions. By integrating emotional intelligence into AI systems, machines can better understand and interact with humans, leading to more personalized and effective experiences. This development marks a significant shift in the evolution of AI, moving beyond purely analytical capabilities towards a more holistic understanding of human behavior and communication. As AI continues to become more integrated into various aspects of society, the ability to empathize and adapt to human emotions will be crucial for fostering trust and acceptance of these technologies. The development of emotionally intelligent AI opens up new possibilities for enhancing mental health support, customer service, and interpersonal communication. Machines equipped with emotional intelligence can detect patterns in human emotions, offering tailored responses and interventions to better meet individual needs. In healthcare, for example, emotionally intelligent AI can provide empathetic support to patients, offering comfort and guidance in times of distress. Similarly, in customer service interactions, AI systems can better understand and address customer concerns, leading to improved satisfaction and loyalty. By incorporating emotional intelligence into AI, we are not only advancing technology but also enhancing human-machine collaboration and connection. The development of emotionally intelligent AI also raises ethical concerns regarding privacy, autonomy, and manipulation. As AI systems become more adept at understanding and responding to human emotions, there is the potential for exploitation and misuse of this information. The ability of AI to manipulate emotions and influence decision-making poses significant risks to individuals and society as a whole. The reliance on emotionally intelligent AI in critical areas such as healthcare and finance raises questions about accountability and transparency in algorithmic decision-making. As we navigate the complexities of integrating emotional intelligence into AI, it is essential to prioritize ethical considerations and regulatory frameworks to ensure that these technologies are developed and used responsibly for the benefit of all.

Applications of AI in mental health support

In the realm of mental health support, applications of AI are making significant strides in enhancing the quality and accessibility of care. One key area where AI is being applied is in the early detection of mental health disorders. By analyzing patterns in speech, text, and behavior, AI algorithms can flag potential indicators of conditions such as depression and anxiety. This proactive approach allows for timely intervention, leading to improved outcomes for individuals struggling with mental health issues. AI-powered chatbots and virtual therapists are providing round-the-clock support to those in need, offering a confidential and judgment-free space for individuals to express their thoughts and feelings. AI is revolutionizing the personalization of treatment plans for mental health patients. Machine learning algorithms can analyze vast amounts of data to create tailored interventions that take into account an individuals unique characteristics and needs. This level of customization ensures that treatment approaches are more effective and efficient, ultimately leading to better outcomes for patients. AI-driven tools are empowering mental health professionals by providing them with real-time insights and recommendations based on evidence-based practices, further enhancing the quality of care delivered to patients. AI is breaking down barriers to mental health support by reaching populations that may have limited access to traditional services. Through telehealth platforms and mobile applications, individuals in remote areas or with busy schedules can easily connect with mental health resources. AI algorithms can analyze data from these interactions to continuously improve the services offered, making mental health support more responsive and adaptive to the diverse needs of users. As AI continues to evolve in the mental health arena, it has the potential to transform the way we approach and address mental health challenges, offering new possibilities for early intervention, personalized care, and increased accessibility to support services.

Ethical considerations in AI's role in emotional well-being

AIs role in emotional well-being brings up complex ethical considerations that must be carefully addressed. As AI becomes more advanced and plays a larger role in society, there is a growing concern about its impact on human emotions and mental health. AI systems that can detect and respond to emotions may provide valuable support in areas like mental health care or education. There are concerns about privacy, trust, and the potential for AI to manipulate or exploit emotional vulnerabilities. Its essential to establish clear guidelines and regulations to ensure that AI technologies are used ethically and responsibly in the context of emotional well-being. One major ethical consideration is the potential for bias and discrimination in AI algorithms designed to assess or respond to emotions. If these systems are not carefully programmed and tested, they could inadvertently perpetuate harmful stereotypes or marginalize certain groups. There is the issue of consent and transparency when it comes to AI accessing and analyzing personal emotional data. Users must have control over their data and be fully informed about how it will be used to protect their emotional well-being and privacy. Ethical guidelines and standards must be established to govern the development and implementation of AI technologies in emotional contexts. The integration of AI into emotional well-being services raises questions about the responsibility and accountability of AI developers and operators. In cases where AI systems are providing emotional support or therapy, there must be clear lines of accountability in case of errors or harm. Transparency in how AI algorithms make decisions that impact emotional well-being is crucial to building trust with users. Ethical considerations in AIs role in emotional well-being require a comprehensive approach that considers the potential risks, benefits, and safeguards needed to protect individuals emotional health in an increasingly AI-driven world.

XVIII. AI AND URBAN PLANNING

As AI continues to advance, its impact on urban planning becomes increasingly significant. AI can optimize transportation systems, predict infrastructure needs, and improve city services. By analyzing vast amounts of data, AI can help planners make informed decisions to create more efficient and sustainable cities. AI can be used to analyze traffic patterns and suggest improvements to reduce congestion and emissions. It can also predict population growth and recommend where to focus urban development to accommodate future needs. By integrating AI into urban planning processes, cities can become smarter, more responsive, and better equipped to handle the challenges of a growing population and evolving technological landscape. AI has the potential to revolutionize the way cities are designed and built. Through the use of AI-powered design tools, urban planners can create more innovative and environmentally friendly structures. These tools can generate complex models and simulations that help architects and builders optimize energy usage, improve structural integrity, and enhance overall functionality. AI can also streamline the permitting process by identifying potential conflicts or issues early in the design phase, saving time and reducing costs. By harnessing the power of AI in urban planning, cities can become more sustainable, resilient, and adaptive to the needs of their residents. As AI becomes more integrated into the fabric of urban planning, ethical considerations must be addressed. Issues such as data privacy, algorithm bias, and the displacement of human workers need to be carefully managed to ensure that AI benefits society as a whole. Transparency in the use of AI technologies, accountability for decision-making processes, and the equitable distribution of AI-generated benefits are essential for creating ethical and responsible urban spaces. By establishing clear guidelines and frameworks for the ethical use of AI in urban planning, cities can harness the full potential of this technology while safeguarding the well-being and rights of their citizens.

Smart city initiatives powered by AI

In the realm of smart city initiatives, AI plays a pivotal role in optimizing urban processes and enhancing the quality of life for citizens. By harnessing the power of AI-driven technologies, cities can effectively manage resources, improve transportation systems, and enhance public safety. AI-powered sensors can collect and analyze real-time data, allowing for more efficient traffic flow and reduced energy consumption. Smart city initiatives powered by AI can help in predicting and mitigating potential challenges such as natural disasters or public health crises, enabling proactive decision-making and swift responses. AI facilitates the creation of smart infrastructure that adapts to the needs of a dynamic urban environment. By integrating AI algorithms into city planning and development, municipalities can optimize land use, reduce waste, and promote sustainable practices. AI can optimize waste management systems by predicting collection needs based on historical data and current conditions, leading to a more cost-effective and environmentally friendly approach. AI-driven smart grids can monitor energy consumption patterns and adjust supply accordingly, promoting energy efficiency and reducing carbon emissions. The integration of AI into smart city initiatives represents a significant step towards building more sustainable, efficient, and resilient urban environments. As AI technologies continue to evolve, cities have the opportunity to leverage data-driven insights to improve infrastructure, enhance services, and address complex challenges. It is crucial to prioritize ethical considerations, data privacy, and inclusivity in the implementation of AI-powered solutions to ensure that smart cities benefit all citizens equitably. By fostering collaboration between technology experts, policymakers, and communities, smart city initiatives powered by AI can pave the way for a more connected, intelligent, and sustainable future.

AI in transportation and infrastructure management

AI has already started to revolutionize transportation and infrastructure management by optimizing efficiency and safety. In the realm of transportation, AI-powered systems are being used to analyze traffic patterns, optimize routes, and even assist in autonomous driving technology. These advancements are not only improving the overall commuter experience but also reducing traffic congestion and emissions. For infrastructure management, AI is proving to be vital in predicting maintenance needs, optimizing energy consumption, and enhancing overall performance. By utilizing AI, authorities can make more informed decisions, leading to cost savings and increased sustainability in infrastructure projects. One key aspect of AI in transportation and infrastructure management is its ability to collect and analyze vast amounts of data in real-time. This data-driven approach enables predictive maintenance, which can help prevent costly breakdowns and downtime in transportation systems and infrastructure. AI algorithms can detect patterns and anomalies that may not be obvious to human operators, allowing for proactive measures to be taken. This data-driven decision-making process empowers transportation and infrastructure managers to allocate resources effectively and prioritize maintenance tasks based on actual need, improving overall system reliability and longevity. In addition to enhancing efficiency, AI in transportation and infrastructure management also plays a crucial role in enhancing safety and security. By leveraging AI-powered sensors and monitoring systems, transportation agencies can detect potential hazards, predict risks, and even prevent accidents before they occur. Similarly, in infrastructure management, AI can assist in identifying structural weaknesses, monitoring environmental impacts, and ensuring compliance with safety regulations. These safety measures not only protect the general public but also contribute to the overall resilience and sustainability of transportation systems and infrastructure networks.

Ethical considerations in AI-driven urban development

In the realm of AI-driven urban development, one of the most pressing issues is the ethical considerations that must be taken into account. As cities increasingly rely on AI to optimize transportation, energy usage, and public services, questions of privacy, equity, and autonomy come to the forefront. When implementing AI systems to manage traffic flow, decisions on prioritizing certain routes or vehicles can lead to unintended consequences such as exacerbating existing inequalities. Ensuring that these systems are designed with the values of fairness and transparency is crucial to prevent any negative impacts on vulnerable populations. The deployment of AI in urban development raises concerns about data privacy and surveillance. With the vast amounts of data being collected and analyzed to improve city operations, there is a risk of infringing on individuals privacy rights. Striking a balance between using data for the public good and protecting personal information is a delicate task that requires strict regulations and oversight. The potential for misuse of AI-powered surveillance systems to infringe on civil liberties highlights the need for robust ethical guidelines to safeguard against abuse. In navigating the complexities of AI-driven urban development, stakeholders must also consider the implications of automation on employment and economic stability. As AI systems increasingly take over tasks traditionally carried out by humans, there is a possibility of widespread job displacement and income inequality. Ensuring that the benefits of AI are equitably distributed and that mechanisms are in place to support those affected by automation will be essential in fostering a sustainable and inclusive future for cities. By addressing these ethical considerations proactively, policymakers and developers can pave the way for a more ethical and responsible integration of AI in urban environments.

XIX. AI AND THE FUTURE OF WORK

In the realm of work, AI is poised to revolutionize industries, creating both opportunities and challenges for labor markets worldwide. As AI technologies continue to advance, the nature of work is likely to undergo significant transformations, with tasks being automated and new job roles emerging to leverage the capabilities of intelligent machines. This shift towards a more automated workforce raises important questions about the future of human employment, as well as the skills and competencies required to thrive in an AI-driven economy. The integration of AI into the workplace has implications for productivity, efficiency, and innovation. Automation can streamline processes, reduce errors, and increase overall output, leading to enhanced competitiveness for businesses. This also raises concerns about job displacement and the need for reskilling and upskilling to ensure that workers are prepared for the evolving job market. As AI becomes more sophisticated, organizations will need to adapt their workforce strategies to harness the benefits of automation while mitigating the potential negative impacts on employees. In order to navigate this transformative period, policymakers, businesses, and educational institutions will need to collaborate to develop comprehensive strategies that address the challenges posed by AI in the future of work. This includes fostering a culture of lifelong learning, fostering creativity and critical thinking, and promoting adaptability to technological change. By investing in education and training programs that equip individuals with the skills needed to thrive in an AI-driven economy, society can harness the full potential of AI while ensuring that the benefits are shared equitably across all segments of the population.

Reskilling and upskilling for an AI-driven economy

In the context of the rapid advancement of AI technologies, the importance of reskilling and upskilling the workforce for an AI-driven economy cannot be overstated. As automation continues to reshape industries, workers need to adapt to the changing landscape by acquiring new skills that complement AI systems. Employees in manufacturing may need to learn how to operate and maintain robots, while those in customer service may need to enhance their emotional intelligence to work effectively alongside AI-powered chatbots. This shift in skill requirements necessitates continuous learning and development to ensure employability in the future job market. Reskilling and upskilling programs play a crucial role in mitigating potential job displacement caused by automation. By providing workers with the necessary training to transition into roles that leverage AI technologies, these programs can help individuals stay relevant and competitive in the labor market. Governments, businesses, and educational institutions must collaborate to design and implement effective reskilling initiatives that cater to the needs of various industries and demographics. Investing in lifelong learning opportunities and career development pathways can empower workers to navigate the challenges posed by the AI-driven economy and secure stable employment in the face of technological disruption. In addition to individual readiness, the reskilling and upskilling of the workforce contribute to the overall socioeconomic resilience required for a successful transition to an AI-driven economy. A skilled and adaptable workforce not only drives innovation and productivity but also fosters economic growth and social cohesion. By equipping workers with the skills to harness AI technologies effectively, organizations can unlock new opportunities for value creation and sustainable development. Reskilling and upskilling initiatives should be seen as an investment in human capital that not only prepares individuals for the future of work but also strengthens the foundations of a thriving AI-powered society.

Human-AI collaboration in the workplace

In the modern workplace, the collaboration between humans and AI has become increasingly common and essential. AI systems are designed to complement human skills and enhance productivity by performing repetitive tasks more efficiently, processing vast amounts of data, and providing valuable insights for decision-making. This partnership allows employees to focus on more creative and complex aspects of their work, while AI handles routine operations. By leveraging the unique strengths of both humans and AI, organizations can achieve higher levels of innovation and competitiveness. With the integration of AI in the workplace, there is a shift towards a more dynamic and adaptive environment where human-AI collaboration is redefining traditional job roles. Individuals are required to develop new skills such as data analysis, problem-solving, and critical thinking to effectively work alongside AI technologies. This evolution demands a flexible mindset and a willingness to embrace change, as employees navigate the complexities of interacting with intelligent machines. Organizations must invest in training programs to empower their workforce with the necessary knowledge and capabilities to leverage AI tools effectively. Despite the many advantages of human-AI collaboration in the workplace, there are also challenges that need to be addressed. One of the key concerns is ensuring the ethical use of AI systems, including issues related to privacy, bias, and transparency. Organizations must establish clear guidelines and standards for the responsible deployment of AI technologies to safeguard against unintended consequences. There is a need to maintain a balance between the automation of tasks and the preservation of human jobs, ensuring that AI enhances rather than replaces human capabilities. By fostering a harmonious relationship between humans and AI, the workplace can evolve into a more efficient, innovative, and inclusive environment.

Socioeconomic implications of AI on employment and income distribution

The socioeconomic implications of AI on employment and income distribution are multifaceted, with both opportunities and challenges arising from the integration of advanced technologies into various industries. On one hand, AI has the potential to increase productivity, streamline processes, and drive innovation, leading to economic growth and job creation in new sectors. There is also concern about the displacement of workers in traditional roles as automation replaces manual tasks. This shift could widen income inequality, as jobs requiring higher levels of education and technical skills become more lucrative while low-skilled workers face a decline in demand. The impact of AI on employment extends beyond individual job roles to the structure of the workforce as a whole. The rise of AI-powered systems could lead to a restructuring of job hierarchies, with some positions becoming obsolete while others require adaptation to work alongside machines effectively. This transformation could result in a polarization of the labor market, where highly skilled workers benefit from AI advancements while those with limited access to education and training struggle to compete in an automated economy. As a result, policymakers must consider strategies to ensure a fair distribution of the benefits of AI, such as investing in upskilling programs and implementing policies to support workers in transitioning to new roles. The socioeconomic implications of AI on employment and income distribution underscore the importance of proactive measures to mitigate potential inequalities and disruptions. As AI technology continues to advance, it is crucial for stakeholders at all levels – from governments and businesses to educational institutions and individuals – to collaborate on finding solutions that promote inclusivity and equity in the workforce. By fostering a culture of lifelong learning, supporting career transitions, and promoting social safety nets, societies can harness the potential of AI to foster economic growth while ensuring that the benefits are shared by all members of the workforce, creating a more sustainable and equitable future for generations to come.

XX. AI AND ETHICAL DECISION-MAKING

The integration of AI into decision-making processes has raised significant ethical considerations that cannot be overlooked. As AI algorithms become increasingly powerful and autonomous, they have the potential to shape crucial aspects of our lives, from healthcare to criminal justice. The issue lies in ensuring that these algorithms prioritize ethical values and principles, such as fairness, transparency, and accountability. Without a clear ethical framework guiding AI development and deployment, there is a risk of perpetuating bias, discrimination, and harm in the decisions made by these systems. It is essential for organizations and policymakers to actively engage in discussions on AI ethics to safeguard against negative societal impacts. The complexity of AI systems poses challenges in understanding and interpreting the reasoning behind their decisions, known as the black box problem. This opacity can lead to concerns regarding accountability and responsibility when errors or biases occur. Ethical decision-making requires not only transparency in how AI algorithms operate but also mechanisms for individuals to challenge or appeal decisions that may have adverse effects. Creating mechanisms for explainability and interpretability can enhance trust and confidence in AI systems, ensuring that their decisions align with ethical standards and values. By promoting transparency and accountability, organizations can mitigate ethical risks and promote the responsible use of AI technology in various domains. The rapid evolution of AI technologies demands continuous monitoring and evaluation of their ethical implications to address emerging challenges effectively. As AI systems become more sophisticated and autonomous, the ethical dilemmas they present grow in complexity, requiring dynamic and adaptive ethical guidelines. Establishing interdisciplinary collaborations between ethicists, technologists, policymakers, and other stakeholders can foster a holistic approach to addressing ethical concerns in AI development and deployment. By fostering open dialogue and collaboration, society can proactively address ethical challenges and ensure that AI technologies align with human values and priorities. The pursuit of ethical decision-making in AI requires a concerted effort from all stakeholders to uphold ethical principles and promote responsible innovation in the field.

Moral reasoning in AI systems

The issue of moral reasoning in AI systems is a pivotal aspect that must be carefully considered as technology advances towards higher levels of artificial intelligence. The ability of AI to make ethical decisions raises concerns about the potential consequences of automated systems acting with autonomy in situations where ethical dilemmas arise. Without a solid framework for incorporating moral principles into AI algorithms, there is a risk of unintended outcomes that may conflict with human values. It is essential to develop mechanisms that allow AI systems to interpret and apply moral reasoning in a way that aligns with ethical standards. In this context, the field of machine ethics has emerged as a critical area of research, aiming to imbue AI systems with the capacity to make moral judgments and act ethically in diverse scenarios. By integrating moral reasoning models into AI algorithms, developers seek to ensure that machines can navigate complex moral dilemmas and make decisions that reflect human values. This approach involves encoding ethical principles and rules into the systems decision-making processes, enabling it to evaluate the implications of its actions from a moral standpoint. The goal is to create AI systems that can act in accordance with ethical norms and contribute positively to society. The integration of moral reasoning in AI systems not only raises technical challenges but also poses philosophical questions about the nature of moral agency in machines. As AI becomes more sophisticated, it prompts a reevaluation of what it means to attribute moral responsibility to non-human entities. The development of autonomous AI systems capable of moral reasoning blurs the line between human and machine agency, leading to discussions about accountability and the implications of delegating ethical decisions to intelligent machines. These reflections underscore the need for a multidisciplinary approach that encompasses not only technical expertise but also ethical considerations and philosophical reflections on the intersection of AI and moral reasoning.

Ethical frameworks for AI programming

In the realm of AI programming, ethical frameworks play a crucial role in guiding the development and deployment of advanced technology. One key aspect is the concept of transparency, ensuring that the inner workings of AI systems are understandable to users and developers alike. By promoting transparency, ethical frameworks can help build trust in AI technologies and mitigate potential risks associated with their deployment. Ethical guidelines can address issues such as bias in AI algorithms, ensuring that decision-making processes are fair and equitable. These frameworks serve as a roadmap for developers, emphasizing the importance of ethical considerations in all stages of AI programming. Another important aspect of ethical frameworks for AI programming is the principle of accountability. Developers must be held responsible for the outcomes of their AI systems, ensuring that they are designed and implemented in a way that aligns with ethical standards. By establishing clear lines of accountability, ethical frameworks can help prevent potential harm caused by AI technologies. Accountability mechanisms can incentivize developers to prioritize ethical considerations throughout the programming process, ultimately leading to more responsible AI systems. This emphasis on accountability reinforces the idea that ethical frameworks are essential for guiding the responsible development of AI technology. Ethical frameworks can promote the principle of beneficence in AI programming, ensuring that the ultimate goal of AI systems is to benefit society as a whole. By prioritizing the well-being of individuals and society, ethical guidelines can steer the development of AI technology towards positive outcomes. This can involve considerations such as privacy protection, data security, and respect for user autonomy. By adhering to the principle of beneficence, AI programmers can contribute to the advancement of technology in a way that enhances human welfare and promotes societal good. In essence, ethical frameworks serve as a foundational tool for ensuring that AI programming aligns with the values and principles that are important for the well-being of society.

Accountability and transparency in AI decision-making
Accountability and transparency in AI decision-making are cru-

cial aspects that must be addressed as we approach the technological singularity. With AI systems gaining the ability to make complex decisions independently, it becomes essential to establish mechanisms that ensure accountability for their actions. This involves defining clear lines of responsibility for the outcomes generated by AI algorithms, as well as implementing processes to trace and audit the decision-making process. Without such accountability measures in place, the risks of unintended consequences or biased results increase significantly, jeopardizing the trust and acceptance of AI technologies in society. Transparency in AI decision-making is equally important, as it provides insight into the inner workings of algorithms and the factors influencing their outputs. By understanding how AI arrives at its decisions, stakeholders can evaluate the reliability and fairness of the results, leading to increased trust and confidence in the technology. Transparent AI systems also facilitate the identification and mitigation of biases that may inadvertently shape decision outcomes. Through transparency, users can gain visibility into the data inputs, algorithms, and processes used by AI systems, enabling them to assess the validity and ethical implications of the decisions made. To achieve accountability and transparency in AI decision-making, it is essential to establish comprehensive guidelines and standards that govern the development and deployment of AI technologies. Regulatory frameworks should outline the responsibilities of AI developers, users, and supervisory bodies, specifying criteria for evaluating the ethical and legal implications of AI decisions. Mechanisms for monitoring and enforcing compliance with these standards must be put in place to ensure that AI systems operate in a manner that upholds societal values and norms. By fostering a culture of accountability and transparency, we can harness the potential of AI while mitigating the risks associated with its unchecked proliferation.

XXI. AI IN EDUCATION AND LEARNING

In the realm of education and learning, the integration of AI has the potential to revolutionize traditional teaching methods. With AI-powered tools, educators can personalize learning experiences, adapting the curriculum to each students pace and needs. These smart systems can provide instant feedback, allowing students to track their progress in real-time and make necessary adjustments to enhance their learning outcomes. By harnessing the power of AI, educational institutions can optimize their resources, improve efficiency, and tailor education to meet the demands of the modern digital era. AI technology can facilitate a more interactive and engaging learning environment, fostering critical thinking, creativity, and problem-solving skills among students. Virtual reality simulations, intelligent tutoring systems, and online platforms powered by AI algorithms offer immersive and dynamic learning experiences that transcend traditional classroom constraints. Through AI, students can access a wealth of educational resources and tools at their fingertips, enhancing their ability to explore diverse topics, collaborate with peers, and develop a deeper understanding of complex subjects. By embracing AI in education, institutions can unlock new possibilities for creating a more inclusive and effective learning ecosystem. As AI continues to reshape the educational landscape, it is important to consider the ethical implications and societal impact of these technological advancements. Concerns about data privacy, algorithm bias, and the potential for AI to replace human educators must be addressed through thoughtful regulation and ethical guidelines. Educators, policymakers, and technologists must collaborate to ensure that AI is deployed responsibly, with a focus on enhancing learning outcomes, promoting equity, and safeguarding the well-being of students. By navigating the complex intersection of AI and education with a clear ethical framework, we can harness the transformative power of technology to create a more equitable and accessible education system for all learners.

Personalized learning through AI

AI has the potential to revolutionize personalized learning in education. Through the use of algorithms and data analysis, AI systems can create customized learning paths for each student, catering to their individual learning styles and pace. This personalized approach can greatly improve student engagement and comprehension, as the material is presented in a way that resonates with them. AI can provide real-time feedback to both students and teachers, allowing for immediate adjustments to be made to optimize the learning process. AI can also assist in identifying areas where students may be struggling and offer additional resources or support to address these challenges. By analyzing vast amounts of data on student performance, AI can pinpoint specific areas of weakness and provide targeted interventions to help students overcome obstacles. This proactive approach to personalized learning can prevent students from falling behind and ensure that they receive the support they need to succeed. In addition to enhancing the learning experience for students, AI can also benefit educators by streamlining administrative tasks and providing valuable insights into student performance. By automating routine tasks such as grading and lesson planning, teachers can focus more on individualized instruction and mentorship. AI can also help educators identify trends in student data, allowing them to tailor their teaching strategies to better meet the needs of their students. Personalized learning through AI has the potential to transform the education landscape, creating more engaging and effective learning experiences for students while supporting teachers in their crucial role as facilitators of knowledge.

AI tutors and educational assistants

The integration of AI tutors and educational assistants in the realm of education has shown promising results in terms of personalized learning experiences. These intelligent systems can adapt to individual student needs, offering tailored feedback and guiding students through challenging concepts at their own pace. By leveraging machine learning algorithms, AI tutors can analyze vast amounts of data to identify each student's strengths and weaknesses, allowing for a more targeted approach to education. This personalized feedback fosters a deeper understanding of the material and can ultimately lead to improved academic performance. AI tutors can also play a crucial role in addressing educational disparities by providing access to high-quality instruction for students in underserved communities. With the ability to deliver customized lessons based on each student's unique learning style, AI tutors have the potential to level the playing field and ensure that all students receive the support they need to succeed. By expanding access to personalized education, AI tutors can help bridge the gap between privileged and marginalized students, ultimately contributing to a more equitable and inclusive educational system. In addition to enhancing the learning experience for students, AI tutors and educational assistants can also assist teachers by automating administrative tasks and providing valuable insights into student progress. By streamlining routine activities such as grading assignments and tracking attendance, AI tutors can free up teachers' time to focus on more meaningful interactions with their students. The data generated by these intelligent systems can offer valuable feedback on teaching methods and student performance, enabling educators to make informed decisions and tailor their instructional strategies to meet the needs of their students more effectively. By leveraging AI technology in the classroom, teachers can enhance their teaching practices and create a more engaging and personalized learning environment for their students.

Addressing equity and access in AI-enhanced education

In the realm of AI-enhanced education, addressing equity and access is paramount to ensure that all students can benefit from technological advancements. One approach to achieving this is through personalized learning experiences, where AI algorithms can adapt to individual student needs, catering to diverse learning styles and abilities. By tailoring instruction in this way, marginalized groups or students with unique challenges can receive targeted support, ultimately bridging gaps in achievement and fostering inclusivity in the educational landscape. Incorporating AI tools that provide real-time feedback and assessment can empower educators to intervene promptly when students require additional assistance, thus leveling the playing field and promoting equal access to quality education. Integrating AI into education can help address disparities in resources and opportunities across different regions or socio-economic backgrounds.

AI-powered virtual tutors or online learning platforms can offer educational content to students in remote areas where access to traditional schooling may be limited. By leveraging AI technologies in this way, education can be democratized, ensuring that learners from all walks of life have the chance to acquire knowledge and skills essential for success in the digital age. It is crucial to approach the implementation of AI in education thoughtfully, considering ethical implications and potential biases that may inadvertently perpetuate inequities if not carefully monitored and addressed. In striving for equity and access in AI-enhanced education, collaboration between policymakers, educators, technologists, and communities is imperative. Establishing clear guidelines and ethical standards for the development and deployment of AI tools in educational settings can safeguard against unintended consequences and promote fairness. Investing in training programs that equip educators with the knowledge and skills to leverage AI effectively can maximize its benefits and ensure that all students receive a high-quality education. By fostering a culture of inclusivity and accessibility in the realm of AI-enhanced education, society can pave the way for a more equitable and prosperous future for generations to come.

XXII. AI IN AGRICULTURE AND FOOD SECURITY

AI in Agriculture and Food Security has the potential to revolutionize the way we produce and distribute food. By utilizing AI technologies such as drones, sensors, and predictive analytics, farmers can optimize their crop yields, reduce waste, and ensure food quality. AI-powered platforms can monitor soil conditions, weather patterns, and crop health in real-time, providing farmers with valuable insights to make data-driven decisions. This not only improves efficiency but also promotes sustainability by minimizing the use of resources like water and pesticides. AI can play a crucial role in enhancing food security globally. With the worlds population projected to reach 9.7 billion by 2050, there is a growing need for innovative solutions to ensure everyone has access to an adequate and nutritious diet. AI algorithms can help identify food supply chain inefficiencies, predict food shortages, and even assist in developing drought-resistant crop varieties. By harnessing the power of AI in agriculture, we can address food insecurity challenges and work towards achieving a more sustainable and equitable food system for future generations. In addition to its impact on production and distribution, AI in Agriculture and Food Security can also improve food safety and traceability. By implementing AI-powered systems to track food from farm to table, we can quickly identify and contain foodborne illnesses, reducing the risk of outbreaks and protecting public health. With AIs ability to analyze vast amounts of data and detect patterns, we can enhance food quality control measures and ensure that consumers have access to safe and nutritious food options. The integration of AI technologies in the agricultural sector can bring about significant advancements in food security and pave the way for a more sustainable future.

Precision agriculture with AI technologies

Precision agriculture has been revolutionized by the integration of AI technologies, allowing for more efficient and sustainable farming practices. Through the use of sensors, drones, and machine learning algorithms, farmers can now monitor crop health, optimize irrigation, and predict yield with unprecedented accuracy. This level of precision not only maximizes productivity but also reduces waste, environmental impact, and overall operating costs. By leveraging these AI tools, farmers are able to make data-driven decisions in real-time, ensuring that resources are utilized effectively and crops are cultivated with optimal care. One key advantage of AI in precision agriculture is its ability to provide personalized insights and recommendations tailored to specific fields or crops. With the vast amounts of data collected and analyzed by AI systems, farmers can fine-tune their operations to address the unique needs of each plot of land. This customization not only boosts crop yields, but also facilitates the adoption of sustainable practices that promote soil health and biodiversity. By harnessing the power of AI, farmers can achieve a level of precision and efficiency that was previously unimaginable, setting a new standard for modern agriculture. The integration of AI technologies in precision agriculture marks a significant step towards a more connected and intelligent farming ecosystem. Through the utilization of IoT devices and cloud-based platforms, farmers can access real-time data and insights from anywhere, enabling remote monitoring and management of their operations. This interconnected network of smart devices and AI algorithms not only enhances productivity and sustainability but also lays the foundation for a more resilient and adaptive agriculture sector. As AI continues to advance, the potential for further innovations in precision agriculture is vast, promising a future where farmers can cultivate with precision and foresight like never before.

AI applications in food supply chain management

One key area where AI is making significant inroads is in food supply chain management. With the ability to process vast amounts of data quickly and accurately, AI systems can optimize logistics, inventory management, and quality control, leading to improved efficiency and reduced waste in the food industry. AI-powered algorithms can forecast demand based on historical data and current trends, allowing suppliers to adjust production levels accordingly. This not only helps prevent food shortages but also minimizes excess stock, ultimately saving resources and reducing environmental impact. AI applications in food supply chain management can enhance traceability and transparency throughout the entire supply chain. By utilizing blockchain technology, for example, companies can track each step of the production process, from farm to table, ensuring accountability and quality assurance. This level of visibility not only fosters trust between consumers and producers but also enables faster responses to potential food safety issues, ultimately safeguarding public health. In an age where consumers are increasingly concerned about the origin and quality of their food, AI offers a powerful tool to meet these expectations and ensure a more resilient and secure food supply chain. In addition to operational efficiencies and transparency, AI can also play a pivotal role in addressing sustainability challenges in the food industry. By analyzing data on resource usage, carbon footprint, and supply chain emissions, AI systems can help identify opportunities for waste reduction, energy savings, and overall environmental stewardship. With the global population on the rise and natural resources becoming increasingly constrained, leveraging AI technologies in food supply chain management is not only advantageous from a business perspective but also essential for promoting long-term sustainability and resilience in the face of complex challenges such as climate change and food security.

Sustainable farming practices through AI optimization

Sustainable farming practices are being increasingly optimized through the utilization of AI. By implementing AI technologies in agriculture, farmers can benefit from predictive analytics to enhance crop yields, reduce waste, and optimize resource allocation. Machine learning algorithms can analyze vast amounts of data collected from sensors in the field, such as soil moisture levels and weather patterns, to provide real-time insights and recommendations for more efficient farming practices. This level of precision and accuracy allows for the implementation of targeted interventions, ultimately leading to a more sustainable and environmentally friendly approach to farming. AI optimization in sustainable farming practices can contribute to minimizing the use of chemical inputs, such as pesticides and fertilizers. By leveraging AI-driven systems, farmers can implement precision agriculture techniques that target specific areas of the field in need of treatment, rather than applying chemicals uniformly across the entire crop. This not only reduces the environmental impact of farming practices but also improves overall crop health and yield. Through the integration of AI technologies, farmers can move towards a more sustainable model of agriculture that prioritizes ecological balance and long-term viability. The application of AI in sustainable farming practices has the potential to revolutionize the way food is produced and distributed globally. By optimizing resource management, minimizing waste, and increasing productivity, AI-driven solutions can help address food security challenges and ensure a more sustainable agricultural system for future generations. With the use of AI tools, farmers can make informed decisions based on data-driven insights, leading to improved efficiency and profitability. This transformative approach to farming not only benefits individual farmers but also contributes to the larger goal of achieving a more sustainable and resilient food system on a global scale.

XXIII. AI IN LEGAL SYSTEMS

One area where the integration of AI has shown significant potential is in legal systems. AI technologies can sift through vast amounts of data much quicker and more efficiently than humans, aiding in legal research and case analysis. Machine learning algorithms can be used to predict legal outcomes based on precedents, helping lawyers and judges make more informed decisions. AI can assist in contract analysis, flagging potential issues or discrepancies that might have been missed by human eyes. By streamlining these processes, AI can not only save time and resources but also improve the accuracy and consistency of legal assessments. AI in legal systems can also enhance access to justice by providing tools for legal assistance to those who may not be able to afford traditional legal services. Chatbots and virtual legal assistants can guide individuals through legal procedures, explain their rights, and even help in drafting legal documents. This could potentially bridge the gap in legal representation for marginalized communities, leveling the playing field in legal disputes. Concerns regarding data privacy, bias in algorithms, and job displacement in the legal sector need to be addressed to ensure that AI is implemented responsibly and ethically in the legal domain. In the context of the technological singularity, the integration of AI in legal systems raises crucial questions about accountability and oversight. As AI systems become more autonomous and capable of making complex legal decisions, the issue of who is responsible for errors or ethical violations becomes paramount. Establishing clear guidelines and regulations for the deployment of AI in legal proceedings is essential to ensure that human values and rights are upheld. It is imperative that legal frameworks evolve alongside technolog-ical advancements to maintain the integrity and fairness of the legal system in the age of AI. By embracing the potential of AI while also implementing safeguards, the legal sector can lever-age the benefits of automation while upholding the principles of justice and equitable access to legal services.

AI in legal research and case analysis

The integration of AI in legal research and case analysis has revolutionized the field of law. Through advanced algorithms and natural language processing, AI-powered systems can sift through massive amounts of legal documents and precedents at a speed and accuracy far beyond human capabilities. By ana-lyzing patterns and trends, AI can provide valuable insights for lawyers and judges, helping them to make more informed deci-sions. This efficiency not only saves time but also enhances the quality and depth of legal analysis, ultimately leading to more robust legal arguments and outcomes. AI tools can assist in pre-dicting case outcomes based on historical data and legal inter-pretations, offering valuable guidance to legal practitioners. By leveraging machine learning techniques, these systems can identify relevant precedents and statutes, streamline the re-search process, and even generate predictive models for various legal scenarios. This predictive capability can significantly ben-efit legal professionals in preparing arguments, assessing risks, and developing strategies for their cases. AI can enhance the accessibility of legal information and expertise, leveling the playing field for individuals and organizations with limited re-sources, thereby promoting fairness and justice in the legal sys-tem. The incorporation of AI in legal research and case analysis represents a major advancement in the legal profession. By harnessing the power of machine learning and natural language processing, AI systems can augment human decision-making, improve legal research efficiency, and enhance the overall quality of legal services. As these technologies continue to evolve and mature, it is crucial for legal professionals to embrace AI tools as valuable allies in their practice, helping them navigate the complexities of modern legal challenges with greater efficiency and effectiveness. AI in legal research and case analysis holds the potential to reshape the legal landscape, making legal services more accessible, efficient, and equitable for all stakeholders.

Automated contract review and drafting

Automated contract review and drafting have emerged as key applications of AI in the legal sector. By utilizing machine learning algorithms, these tools can efficiently analyze large volumes of legal documents, identify key clauses, and even generate initial drafts. This technology not only saves time for lawyers but also enhances the accuracy and consistency of contract review processes. Automated contract drafting can help streamline negotiations by providing real-time feedback on proposed changes, leading to quicker deal closures. As AI continues to advance, we can expect further improvements in contract management, ultimately transforming the legal landscape. The adoption of automated contract review and drafting tools raises important ethical and regulatory considerations. As AI systems become more sophisticated, issues surrounding accountability and transparency come to the forefront. It is essential to establish clear guidelines for the use of AI in legal processes to ensure that decisions made by these systems align with legal standards and ethical principles. Safeguards must be put in place to protect sensitive information and uphold client confidentiality. By addressing these challenges proactively, the legal industry can capitalize on the benefits of AI while mitigating risks associated with its implementation. In the context of the technological singularity, automated contract review and drafting represent a significant step towards the integration of AI into various aspects of society. As these tools become more prevalent, it becomes crucial for legal professionals to adapt to this changing landscape. Embracing AI can lead to increased efficiency and productivity, but it also requires a level of understanding and oversight to ensure that the technology is used responsibly. By navigating the complexities of AI integration thoughtfully, the legal industry can leverage its potential to drive innovation and enhance the delivery of legal services.

Ethical considerations in AI-assisted legal decision-making

In AI-assisted legal decision-making, ethical considerations play a crucial role in ensuring fairness and accountability. One key issue is transparency, as AI algorithms often operate as black boxes, making it difficult to understand how they arrive at certain conclusions. This lack of transparency can lead to unequal or biased outcomes, particularly in sensitive legal matters. It is essential to establish clear guidelines for the development and use of AI in the legal field, ensuring that decisions are explainable and unbiased. By incorporating transparency into the design of AI systems, legal professionals can better trust and validate the results generated by these technologies. Another ethical consideration in AI-assisted legal decision-making is the potential for unintended consequences. AI algorithms are trained on historical data, which may contain biases or errors that can perpetuate discrimination in decision-making processes. If past legal rulings were biased against certain demographic groups, AI systems trained on this data may continue to produce discriminatory outcomes. Addressing such issues requires a comprehensive review of training data and ongoing monitoring of AI systems to detect and rectify any bias. By proactively identifying and mitigating unintended consequences, the legal community can ensure that AI technologies uphold ethical standards and promote fairness in decision-making. The ethical implications of AI in the legal field extend to questions of responsibility and accountability. Who is ultimately responsible for the decisions made by AI systems in legal contexts? Should developers, users, or the algorithms themselves be held accountable for any errors or harm caused by AI-assisted decisions? These complex questions highlight the need for a framework that clearly delineates roles and responsibilities in AI-assisted legal decision-making. Establishing clear lines of accountability can help prevent potential misuse or abuse of AI technologies, ensuring that ethical standards are upheld and legal outcomes are just and equitable. By addressing these ethical considerations, the legal community can harness the benefits of AI while minimizing the risks associated with its implementation.

XXIV. AI IN SPORTS AND PERFORMANCE ANALYSIS

In the realm of sports and performance analysis, AI has opened up new avenues for athletes, coaches, and teams to enhance their capabilities and strategies. By leveraging AI algorithms and machine learning techniques, vast amounts of data can be processed in real-time to provide valuable insights into athlete performance, injury prevention, and game strategies. AI-powered cameras can track player movements, analyze biomechanics, and predict potential injuries based on movement patterns, allowing teams to make informed decisions about training and game-time strategies. This sophisticated level of analysis not only improves performance but also reduces the risk of injuries, ultimately benefiting the athletes and the team as a whole. AI-driven performance analysis can revolutionize scouting processes by identifying talent at an early stage and predicting future success based on data-driven insights. Coaches and scouts can utilize AI algorithms to assess player skills, cognitive abilities, and potential for growth, giving them a competitive edge in talent acquisition and player development. By identifying key performance indicators and trends, AI can help optimize training programs, customize player development plans, and improve overall team performance. This data-driven approach to talent identification and development not only saves time and resources but also ensures that teams have a well-rounded understanding of their players capabilities and potential. AI in sports can enhance the fan experience by providing real-time insights, interactive experiences, and personalized content. AI-powered platforms can analyze vast amounts of data to deliver personalized content to fans, such as highlights, statistics, and predictive insights. This level of engagement not only increases fan loyalty but also generates new revenue streams for sports organizations. By leveraging AI technologies, sports teams can create immersive fan experiences, optimize marketing strategies, and foster long-term relationships with their audience. This symbiotic relationship between AI, sports, and fans highlights the transformative potential of technology in enhancing the overall sports ecosystem.

AI in sports training and performance optimization

AI is revolutionizing sports training and performance optimization by providing athletes and coaches with unprecedented insights and analysis. Machine learning algorithms can process vast amounts of data, from player performance metrics to game tactics, to identify patterns and trends that can lead to significant improvements. AI-powered systems can track an athletes movements in real-time, offering instant feedback on technique and suggesting personalized training programs tailored to individual strengths and weaknesses. This level of personalized guidance can help athletes reach their full potential and optimize their performance like never before. AI technology is enhancing injury prevention and recovery strategies in sports by monitoring athletes biometric data and predicting potential risks. By analyzing factors such as fatigue levels, heart rate variability, and biomechanics, AI algorithms can alert coaches and medical staff to signs of overtraining or injury susceptibility before they become serious issues. This proactive approach not only minimizes downtime for athletes but also contributes to long-term sustainability and career longevity. In this way, AI is not only improving performance on the field but also safeguarding the health and well-being of athletes off the field. The use of AI in sports has extended beyond individual player analysis to team strategy and game planning. By simulating countless game scenarios and optimizing plays based on data-driven insights, AI can help coaches make more informed decisions during matches. This strategic advantage can be crucial in high-stakes competitions, where split-second choices can determine the outcome of a game. As AI continues to evolve and refine its predictive capabilities, it is reshaping the way sports are approached, coached, and played at all levels, setting new standards for excellence and innovation in the industry.

Data analytics and predictive modeling in sports

Taking a closer look at the impact of data analytics and predictive modeling in sports, it becomes evident that these technologies are revolutionizing the way athletes train, teams strategize, and fans engage with the game. By analyzing vast amounts of data, from player performance statistics to game conditions, coaches and analysts can gain valuable insights into patterns and trends that were previously elusive. This data-driven approach not only enhances player and team performance but also enriches the overall fan experience by providing in-depth analysis and predictions. Data analytics and predictive modeling in sports have the potential to level the playing field by democratizing access to crucial information. With the help of advanced algorithms and machine learning techniques, smaller or less resourceful teams can now compete with larger and more established ones on a more even ground. This has the dual effect of promoting fairness within the industry while also pushing the boundaries of innovation as teams seek new ways to gain a competitive edge. The transformative power of these technologies is reshaping traditional paradigms in sports, leading to a more dynamic and evolving landscape. In addition to improving performance and competitiveness, the integration of data analytics and predictive modeling in sports raises ethical considerations regarding the use of personal data and privacy. As the amount of data collected on athletes and fans continues to grow, questions arise about who has access to this information, how it is used, and the potential implications for individual privacy rights. It is crucial for sports organizations to establish clear guidelines and ethical standards to ensure that these technologies are employed responsibly and accountably, safeguarding the rights and well-being of all stakeholders involved in the sports ecosystem.

Ethical implications of AI in sports competition

One of the domains where the ethical implications of AI are particularly relevant is in sports competition. As AI technology becomes more integrated into sports, questions arise regarding fairness, privacy, and the potential for performance-enhancing capabilities. The use of AI-powered analytics in scouting and player performance evaluation may provide an unfair advantage to teams with greater resources. This raises concerns about equity in sports competition, as well as the need for regulations to ensure a level playing field for all athletes. The implementation of AI in sports raises privacy concerns related to the collection and use of athletes data. As AI systems gather vast amounts of information on individual performance and health, questions emerge about who owns this data and how it should be used.

Ensuring that athletes have control over their personal information and that it is used ethically and responsibly is crucial in maintaining trust and integrity in sports. Transparency in the handling of data is essential to address these ethical challenges and prevent potential abuses in the increasingly data-driven sports industry. The use of AI in sports competition could lead to concerns about the authenticity and integrity of the game itself. With the potential for AI to enhance athletes abilities or even replace them with virtual counterparts, the fundamental principles of fair play and human agency may be called into question. As advancements in AI continue to push the boundaries of what is possible in sports, it is critical to establish clear ethical guidelines to ensure that the spirit of competition is upheld and that athletes are not put in compromising positions. By addressing these ethical implications proactively, the sports industry can embrace the benefits of AI while safeguarding the core values that define the essence of sports competition.

XXV. AI IN DISASTER RESPONSE AND MANAGEMENT

In the realm of disaster response and management, AI is increasingly playing a crucial role in improving efficiency and effectiveness. AI-powered systems can analyze vast amounts of data in real-time, enabling faster decision-making in emergency situations. AI can help predict the path of hurricanes or wildfires, allowing authorities to evacuate populations more accurately and timely. AI-driven drones can assess damage after a disaster, providing valuable information to aid response efforts. By leveraging AI technologies, disaster response teams can optimize resource allocation and coordination, ultimately saving more lives and reducing the impact of catastrophes. AI algorithms can enhance early warning systems by detecting patterns and anomalies that human operators might miss. Machine learning models can analyze social media data to identify areas of distress during disasters, enabling targeted response efforts. AI can assist in optimizing supply chain logistics during crises, ensuring that essential resources reach affected areas promptly. By automating repetitive tasks and facilitating data-driven decision-making, AI enables disaster management teams to focus on strategic planning and problem-solving, thereby enhancing overall response capabilities. Despite the clear benefits of integrating AI into disaster response and management, ethical considerations must be closely examined. Issues such as data privacy, algorithm bias, and accountability in decision-making processes need to be addressed to ensure that AI technologies serve the public interest. It is essential to establish ethical guidelines and regulatory frameworks that govern the use of AI in disaster situations, promoting transparency and accountability. By fostering a culture of responsible AI deployment, stakeholders can harness the full potential of these technologies while safeguarding against potential risks and ensuring that human values remain at the forefront of decision-making processes.

AI for early warning systems and disaster prediction

In the realm of disaster prediction and early warning systems, AI has emerged as a powerful tool capable of analyzing vast amounts of data to detect patterns and signals that may indicate an impending catastrophe. By leveraging machine learning algorithms, AI can sift through various data sources such as satellite imagery, social media feeds, and sensor data to provide timely alerts and forecasts. In the case of natural disasters like hurricanes or wildfires, AI can help predict the path of destruction, enabling authorities to evacuate populations at risk and allocate resources more efficiently. The use of AI for early warning systems extends beyond natural disasters to include human-made crises like cyber-attacks or terrorist threats. By monitoring network traffic and analyzing patterns of malicious behavior, AI can detect potential security breaches or impending attacks before they occur. This proactive approach can significantly enhance cybersecurity measures and help prevent devastating disruptions to infrastructure and critical systems. The predictive capabilities of AI in such scenarios have the potential to save lives and safeguard societal stability in the face of increasing digital threats. While AI holds tremendous promise for improving early warning systems and disaster prediction, it is crucial to address ethical considerations and potential limitations. Ensuring transparency and accountability in the development and deployment of AI technologies is paramount to building trust with stakeholders and communities. Safeguards must be put in place to mitigate biases in AI algorithms that could inadvertently propagate harmful outcomes or exacerbate existing vulnerabilities. By navigating these complexities with foresight and responsibility, AI can continue to advance as a reliable ally in safeguarding against unforeseen disasters and supporting collective resilience in an ever-changing world.

Emergency response coordination with AI

One area where the integration of AI is proving to be highly beneficial is in emergency response coordination. With the ability to analyze massive amounts of data in real-time, AI systems can help emergency responders make faster and more informed decisions during crises. AI-powered algorithms can process data from various sources such as social media, sensors, and communication networks to identify patterns and predict where resources are most needed. This can lead to more efficient deployment of personnel and equipment, ultimately saving lives and reducing the impact of disasters on affected communities. AI can assist in improving communication and collaboration among different agencies involved in emergency response. By providing a centralized platform for sharing information and coordinating efforts, AI can help ensure that all stakeholders are on the same page and working towards common goals. This can be particularly crucial in situations where multiple organizations need to work together seamlessly, such as during natural disasters or large-scale emergencies. AI systems can facilitate the exchange of critical information, enable real-time updates, and enhance overall situational awareness, leading to a more coordinated and effective response. While the potential benefits of integrating AI into emergency response coordination are significant, there are also important considerations to take into account. Privacy and data security concerns, ethical implications of AI decision-making, and the need for human oversight to ensure accountability are all critical issues that must be addressed. It is essential for organizations to implement robust policies and protocols to safeguard against potential risks and ensure that AI is used responsibly and ethically in emergency response settings. By striking a balance between leveraging the capabilities of AI and promoting human judgment and control, we can harness the power of technology to enhance emergency preparedness and response efforts.

Ethical considerations in AI deployment during crises

In the deployment of AI during crises, ethical considerations play a crucial role in ensuring that decisions made by AI systems align with human values and societal norms. One key ethical concern is the potential for bias in AI algorithms, which can perpetuate existing inequalities or discriminatory practices. In the context of emergency response, an AI system may prioritize certain populations over others based on biased data inputs, resulting in unfair treatment during a crisis. It is essential for developers to implement safeguards against bias, such as diverse training data and regular audits, to uphold ethical standards in AI deployment. Another ethical consideration in AI deployment during crises is the issue of transparency and accountability. As AI systems become more complex and autonomous, it can be challenging to understand how decisions are being made and who is responsible for their outcomes. In a crisis situation, where quick and accurate decisions are vital, transparency is key to ensuring that stakeholders can trust AI systems to act in the best interests of those affected. Establishing clear lines of accountability and transparent decision-making processes can help address ethical concerns and build public confidence in the use of AI during crises. The potential for unintended consequences in AI deployment poses ethical dilemmas that must be carefully considered. While AI systems can offer valuable insights and support in crisis management, there is always a risk of unforeseen outcomes or unintended harm. In the case of using AI for predictive analysis during a natural disaster, there may be unintended negative impacts on vulnerable communities if the predictions are inaccurate or misinterpreted. Ethical frameworks and risk assessment protocols should be in place to anticipate and mitigate potential harms, ensuring that AI deployment during crises prioritizes the well-being and safety of all individuals involved.

XXVI. AI IN RETAIL AND CUSTOMER EXPERIENCE

In the retail sector, the integration of AI technologies has revolutionized the customer experience. Through personalized recommendations based on data analysis, AI can anticipate consumer preferences and tailor offerings to individual tastes. This level of customization not only enhances customer satisfaction but also increases brand loyalty and drives sales. With AI-powered chatbots handling customer inquiries and providing real-time support, retailers can offer round-the-clock assistance, improving overall service quality and efficiency. By harnessing predictive analytics, retailers can optimize inventory management, ensuring products are available when and where they are needed, minimizing stockouts and maximizing profitability. AI enables retailers to implement dynamic pricing strategies, adjusting prices in real-time based on market demand and competitor pricing. This flexibility allows retailers to maximize revenue while remaining competitive in a fast-paced market environment. AI-powered image recognition technology facilitates seamless checkout experiences through cashier-less stores, eliminating the need for traditional point-of-sale systems and streamlining the shopping process. By automating routine tasks, such as inventory counting and shelf restocking, AI frees up human employees to focus on higher-value activities, such as customer engagement and strategic decision-making, ultimately improving operational efficiency and driving business growth. While the integration of AI in retail offers substantial benefits, it also raises concerns regarding data privacy and security. As AI systems collect vast amounts of customer data to deliver personalized experiences, ensuring the protection of sensitive information becomes paramount. Retailers must prioritize cybersecurity measures to safeguard customer data from potential breaches or misuse. Ethical considerations surrounding the use of AI in influencing consumer behavior and decision-making must be carefully addressed to build trust and maintain transparency with customers. By navigating these challenges thoughtfully and responsibly, retailers can harness the full potential of AI to enhance the customer experience while upholding ethical standards and fostering long-term relationships with consumers.

Personalized shopping experiences with AI

AI-enabled personalized shopping experiences have become a game-changer in the retail industry, offering consumers tailored recommendations based on their preferences and past behaviors. By leveraging data analytics and machine learning algorithms, AI can anticipate customer needs and provide relevant product suggestions in real time. This level of personalization not only enhances the shopping experience but also increases sales conversion rates, as customers are more likely to make a purchase when presented with items that align with their individual tastes. AI can streamline the entire shopping journey, from product discovery to checkout, by automating repetitive tasks and simplifying decision-making processes. Virtual shopping assistants powered by AI can assist customers in finding the right products, answering questions, and even processing payments seamlessly. This level of convenience and efficiency not only saves time for consumers but also boosts operational efficiency for retailers, leading to improved customer satisfaction and loyalty. Despite the numerous benefits of AI-driven personalized shopping experiences, there are concerns regarding data privacy and security. As AI algorithms rely on vast amounts of consumer data to deliver personalized recommendations, there is a heightened risk of data breaches and unauthorized access. The ethical implications of using AI to influence consumer behavior and shape purchasing decisions also raise questions about transparency and consent. As AI continues to revolutionize the retail landscape, it is essential for companies to prioritize data protection measures and establish clear guidelines to ensure the ethical use of AI in personalized shopping experiences.

AI-driven inventory management and supply chain optimization

AI-driven inventory management and supply chain optimization have revolutionized the way businesses operate in todays fast-paced global market. By using advanced algorithms and predictive analytics, AI systems can accurately forecast demand, optimize inventory levels, and streamline logistics processes. This has led to significant cost savings for companies and improved customer satisfaction due to better product availability. Companies like Amazon have utilized AI-powered systems to analyze historical sales data, market trends, and even weather forecasts to ensure they have the right products in the right quantity at the right time. One of the key advantages of AI-driven inventory management is its ability to adapt in real-time to changes in demand or supply chain disruptions. Traditional methods often struggle to quickly respond to unexpected events, leading to overstocking or stockouts. AI systems, on the other hand, can continuously monitor data streams and make adjustments on the fly, optimizing inventory levels and minimizing the risk of excess inventory or stock shortages. This agility is crucial in to-days volatile business environment, where companies need to be flexible and responsive to market dynamics to stay competitive. AI-driven inventory management not only enhances operational efficiency but also enables companies to make more strategic business decisions. By providing insights into demand patterns, seasonality, and customer preferences, AI systems can help businesses align their supply chain strategies with market trends and improve overall business performance. This proactive approach allows organizations to anticipate future demand, optimize production schedules, and ultimately increase profitability. As AI technology continues to evolve, the potential for even greater optimization and efficiency gains in inventory and supply chain management will only continue to grow.

Privacy concerns and data security in AI-powered retail

Privacy concerns and data security in AI-powered retail are becoming increasingly prevalent as companies leverage advanced technologies to personalize customer experiences. With the vast amount of data being collected, stored, and analyzed in real-time, there is a growing apprehension about how this information is being used and protected. Customers are rightfully concerned about potential breaches of their personal data and the possibility of it falling into the wrong hands. Retailers must address these privacy concerns by implementing robust security measures, encryption protocols, and transparent data handling practices to build trust with their customers. AI technologies in retail can inadvertently infringe on consumer privacy by utilizing algorithms that target individuals based on their online behavior and preferences. This raises ethical questions about the extent to which companies should be allowed to track and analyze customer data without explicit consent. As AI systems become more sophisticated in predicting consumer behavior, there is a fine line between offering personalized recommendations and invading an individuals privacy. Regulations and guidelines must be established to ensure that data collection and utilization adhere to ethical standards and respect the privacy rights of consumers. In light of these privacy concerns, the integration of AI in retail must prioritize data security and privacy protection measures. Retailers must be transparent about the data they collect, how it is being used, and provide consumers with control over their personal information. Implementing privacy-enhancing technologies such as differential privacy and federated learning can mitigate privacy risks while still extracting valuable insights from data. As technology continues to advance, it is crucial for retailers to uphold ethical standards, prioritize consumer privacy, and foster a culture of trust in the AI-driven retail landscape.

XXVII. AI IN TRANSPORTATION AND AUTONOMOUS VEHICLES

In the realm of transportation, the integration of AI has paved the way for significant advancements, particularly in the development of autonomous vehicles. Through the use of sophisticated algorithms and sensor systems, AI-enabled cars can navigate roads, interpret traffic signals, and react to unpredictable situations with remarkable precision. This technology has the potential to revolutionize the way we commute, offering increased safety, efficiency, and convenience for passengers. As with any disruptive innovation, the widespread adoption of autonomous vehicles raises complex ethical and regulatory considerations that must be carefully addressed. One of the key benefits of AI in transportation is the potential to reduce human error, which is a leading cause of accidents on the road. By relying on algorithms that can process vast amounts of data in real time, autonomous vehicles have the ability to make split-second decisions that prioritize safety and minimize the risk of collisions. This not only enhances the overall driving experience but also has the potential to save countless lives by mitigating the impact of human fallibility. The integration of AI in transportation can help to alleviate traffic congestion and optimize routes, leading to more efficient use of resources and reduced carbon emissions. Despite the promising advancements in AI-enabled transportation, there are also concerns surrounding issues such as data privacy, cybersecurity, and the potential displacement of jobs in the traditional automotive industry. As autonomous vehicles become more prevalent on the roads, there is a need for robust regulatory frameworks to ensure that these technologies are deployed in a manner that prioritizes public safety and respects individual privacy rights. Stakeholders must consider the socioeconomic implications of widespread automation in transportation, including the need for retraining programs to help workers transition to new roles in a rapidly evolving industry. By addressing these challenges proactively, we can harness the full potential of AI in transportation while mitigating its unintended consequences.

AI in traffic management and route optimization

AI in traffic management and route optimization has the potential to revolutionize the way we navigate our cities and transportation networks. By implementing advanced algorithms and real-time data analysis, AI systems can predict traffic patterns, detect bottlenecks, and suggest alternative routes to optimize travel time. This not only reduces congestion and air pollution but also improves overall efficiency in transportation systems. With the integration of AI, traffic management can become more responsive and adaptive to changing conditions, enhancing the overall user experience for commuters and drivers. AI-driven route optimization can have a significant impact on reducing fuel consumption and greenhouse gas emissions. By calculating the most fuel-efficient routes based on a variety of factors such as traffic volume, road conditions, and vehicle performance, AI systems can help minimize the environmental impact of transportation. In a world where sustainability and environmental conservation are paramount, the implementation of AI in traffic management aligns with global efforts to reduce carbon emissions and combat climate change. This not only benefits the environment but also contributes to creating a more sustainable and livable urban environment for future generations. In addition to the environmental and efficiency benefits, AI in traffic management also enhances safety by identifying potential risks and hazards on the road. Through real-time monitoring and analysis of traffic conditions, AI systems can proactively alert drivers to dangers such as accidents, construction zones, or adverse weather conditions. This proactive approach to safety not only reduces the likelihood of accidents but also improves emergency response times, ultimately saving lives. By leveraging AI technology in traffic management and route optimization, cities can create safer, more sustainable, and efficient transportation systems for the benefit of all residents.

Development of autonomous vehicles with AI technology

The development of autonomous vehicles, integrated with advanced AI technology, represents a significant milestone in the evolution of transportation. These vehicles rely on a complex network of sensors, algorithms, and machine learning capabilities to navigate and make decisions in real-time. The implementation of AI in autonomous vehicles allows for adaptive responses to changing road conditions and unexpected obstacles, enhancing overall safety and efficiency on the roads. With the ability to learn from past experiences and improve performance over time, autonomous vehicles are poised to revolutionize the way we travel. In the realm of autonomous vehicles, AI technology plays a crucial role in shaping the future of mobility. The integration of AI enables vehicles to communicate with each other and with smart infrastructure, creating a dynamic and interconnected transportation ecosystem. This interconnectedness has the potential to reduce traffic congestion, increase fuel efficiency, and optimize travel routes, leading to a more sustainable and user-friendly transportation system. As AI continues to evolve, autonomous vehicles are expected to become more reliable, secure, and cost-effective, making them a viable option for mainstream adoption. As autonomous vehicles with AI technology become more prevalent on our roads, it is imperative to address the ethical and regulatory challenges that come with their widespread deployment. Issues such as data privacy, liability in case of accidents, and the impact on traditional transportation industries need to be carefully considered and addressed. Ensuring that these vehicles are programmed with ethical decision-making frameworks and adhere to strict safety standards is essential in building public trust and acceptance. By proactively addressing these issues, we can pave the way for a future where autonomous vehicles coexist harmoniously with other modes of transportation, benefiting society as a whole.

Legal and ethical challenges in AI-driven transportation systems

In AI-driven transportation systems, legal and ethical challenges abound as technology rapidly advances. One major concern is the issue of liability in the case of accidents involving autonomous vehicles. Current laws are not equipped to assign responsibility when AI systems make decisions independently, leaving questions regarding who should be held accountable in the event of harm. There are ethical dilemmas surrounding the programming of AI algorithms, with concerns about biases that may be inadvertently incorporated into decision-making processes. Ensuring that these systems are fair and just in their operations poses a significant challenge for regulators and developers alike. Privacy and data protection are critical issues in AI-driven transportation systems. With the collection of vast amounts of data on individuals movements and preferences, there is a risk of this information being misused or exploited. Ensuring that adequate safeguards are in place to protect user data from breaches or unauthorized access is crucial for maintaining trust in these systems. The potential for surveillance and tracking raises concerns about the erosion of personal freedoms and rights in a society where AI is ubiquitous in transportation. The ethical implications of job displacement in the transportation sector due to automation must be carefully considered. As AI-driven technologies replace traditional roles, there is a risk of widespread unemployment and economic upheaval. Ensuring a smooth transition for workers through retraining and reskilling programs is essential to mitigate the negative impacts of automation on society. Balancing the benefits of AI-driven transportation systems with the preservation of livelihoods and economic stability presents a complex challenge that requires careful planning and proactive measures from policymakers. Addressing these legal and ethical challenges will be crucial in shaping a future where AI-driven transportation systems can coexist harmoniously with society.

XXVIII. AI IN SPACE EXPLORATION

AI in space exploration has the potential to revolutionize our understanding of the universe. From autonomous rovers on Mars to advanced satellite systems monitoring distant planets, AI is enhancing the capabilities of space missions. By integrating AI into spacecraft systems, scientists can analyze data more efficiently, predict equipment failures, and even discover new phenomena previously overlooked by traditional methods. AI enables us to explore environments that are inhospitable to human presence, opening up new opportunities for scientific discovery and innovation in the realm of space exploration. One of the key advantages of using AI in space exploration is its ability to adapt and learn from new situations. Machine learning algorithms can process vast amounts of data in real-time, allowing for rapid decision-making during space missions. This adaptability is crucial in unpredictable environments where conditions can change rapidly, such as landing on a comet or navigating through asteroid fields. With the help of AI, space agencies can explore celestial bodies more effectively and gather valuable information that would be challenging to obtain using traditional methods alone. In addition to enhancing scientific research, AI in space exploration also presents opportunities for sustainable development and resource utilization. By automating tasks such as resource management and navigation, AI can help reduce costs and increase the efficiency of space missions. The data collected by AI-powered systems can provide valuable insights into the potential for future human colonization of other planets. As we continue to push the boundaries of exploration, the integration of AI will play a vital role in expanding our knowledge of the cosmos and unlocking new possibilities for the future of space exploration.

AI applications in space mission planning and execution

AI applications in space mission planning and execution have revolutionized the way we explore the cosmos. By leveraging artificial intelligence, space agencies can analyze vast amounts of data to make informed decisions in real time. Machine learning algorithms can predict potential hazards, optimize trajectory planning, and even assist in autonomous navigation of spacecraft. These advancements not only improve the efficiency of missions but also enhance the safety of astronauts and equipment in the harsh environment of space. AI plays a crucial role in optimizing resource management during space missions. From fuel consumption to power distribution, AI algorithms can optimize resource allocation to ensure the longevity and success of missions. By continuously learning and adapting to changing environments, AI systems can make adjustments on the fly, maximizing the utilization of limited resources in space. This level of automation and adaptability is essential for long-duration missions such as interplanetary travel, where human intervention may be limited or delayed. AI applications are instrumental in enhancing the scientific outcomes of space missions. By analyzing vast amounts of data collected by space probes and telescopes, AI systems can identify patterns, anomalies, and correlations that may go unnoticed by human researchers. This deep learning capability enables scientists to make new discoveries, refine hypotheses, and expand our understanding of the universe. As we continue to push the boundaries of space exploration, AI will undoubtedly play an increasingly vital role in shaping the future of interplanetary travel and scientific discovery.

Robotics and AI in extraterrestrial exploration

Moving beyond Earth, robotics and AI play a crucial role in extraterrestrial exploration. From Mars rovers to autonomous spacecraft, these technologies enable scientists to gather data from distant planets and moons. The precision and efficiency of robotic systems make them ideal for tasks in harsh environments where human presence is impractical or dangerous. AI algorithms can analyze vast amounts of data to uncover hidden patterns, aiding researchers in understanding the mysteries of the cosmos. As humanity aims to expand its reach into the universe, integrating robotics and AI into space exploration becomes essential for discovering new worlds and unraveling the secrets of the universe. The use of robotics and AI in extraterrestrial exploration has the potential to revolutionize our understanding of the universe. With advancements in machine learning and deep neural networks, these technologies can enhance our ability to map distant galaxies, search for habitable exoplanets, and even detect signs of extraterrestrial life. By leveraging robotics and AI, scientists can conduct experiments and collect samples in space with unprecedented precision and accuracy. This capability opens up new avenues for exploring the cosmos and could lead to groundbreaking discoveries that reshape our understanding of the universe and our place within it. The integration of robotics and AI in extraterrestrial exploration raises ethical considerations regarding the impact of these technologies on other planets and potential alien life forms. As we venture into space, it is crucial to establish guidelines and protocols to ensure the responsible use of robotics and AI in exploration missions. Issues such as contamination, interference with indigenous ecosystems, and respect for alien cultures must be carefully addressed to prevent unintended consequences. By developing a framework that encompasses ethical principles and environmental stewardship, we can safeguard the integrity of extraterrestrial environments while advancing our scientific knowledge of the cosmos.

Ethical considerations in AI use in space exploration

In the context of space exploration, the use of AI raises important ethical considerations that must be carefully addressed. When AI is deployed in missions beyond Earth, there is a significant risk of encountering unknown variables and situations that could challenge the preprogrammed algorithms. Ensuring that AI systems are designed to prioritize human safety, adhere to ethical guidelines, and make reliable decisions even in unpredictable environments is crucial to the success of space exploration missions. The potential for AI to interact with extraterrestrial life, if discovered, adds another layer of complexity to the ethical framework that must govern its use in space. One key ethical consideration in the use of AI in space exploration is the issue of autonomy. As AI systems become more sophisticated and capable of independent decision-making, questions arise about accountability and control. Who is ultimately responsible for the actions taken by AI in a space mission? How can we ensure that AI aligns with human values and ethical standards when operating in a distant and potentially hazardous environment? These are complex ethical dilemmas that require careful deliberation and the establishment of clear guidelines to govern the behavior of AI systems in space. The potential for AI systems to reveal sensitive information about Earth or human civilization to extraterrestrial beings raises ethical concerns about privacy and security. As AI technologies advance and become more integrated into space exploration, it is essential to consider the implications of unintentional information disclosure and the need to protect confidential data. Establishing robust protocols for data security and privacy will be essential to prevent unintended consequences that could have far-reaching implications for both humanity and potential extraterrestrial civilizations. The ethical considerations surrounding AI use in space exploration are multifaceted and require careful attention to ensure that the benefits of technology are balanced with the protection of human values and principles.

XXIX. AI IN PHILANTHROPY AND SOCIAL IMPACT

In the realm of philanthropy and social impact, AI has the potential to revolutionize the way organizations address societal challenges. By leveraging AI technologies, philanthropic efforts can be made more efficient and impactful. AI-powered data analytics can help identify areas of need with greater precision, enabling philanthropic organizations to allocate resources more effectively. AI can optimize processes such as donation management and program evaluation, streamlining operations and maximizing the impact of each contribution. Through the integration of AI into philanthropic initiatives, organizations can achieve greater transparency, accountability, and scalability, ultimately leading to more sustainable solutions for social issues. AI can play a crucial role in driving innovation in the philanthropic sector by facilitating collaboration and knowledge sharing among stakeholders. AI-powered platforms can connect donors, non-profit organizations, and beneficiaries, creating a networked ecosystem that fosters collaboration and accelerates the development of innovative solutions. By harnessing the power of AI to facilitate communication and coordination, philanthropic initiatives can leverage collective expertise and resources to address complex challenges more effectively. AI can enable the monitoring and evaluation of social impact projects in real-time, providing valuable insights that can inform decision-making and drive continuous improvement in program delivery. While the potential benefits of AI in philanthropy and social impact are significant, it is crucial to address the ethical and regulatory implications of integrating AI technologies into these sectors. As AI becomes increasingly sophisticated, concerns around data privacy, bias, and autonomy arise, highlighting the need for comprehensive guidelines and regulations to govern its use in philanthropic endeavors. By establishing clear ethical standards and ensuring transparency in AI algorithms and decision-making processes, organizations can mitigate potential risks and uphold the principles of fairness and accountability. The responsible deployment of AI in philanthropy requires a balanced approach that maximizes the benefits of technology while safeguarding the interests and rights of all stakeholders involved.

AI for social good initiatives and humanitarian aid

In recent years, AI for social good initiatives and humanitarian aid have gained traction as powerful tools to address complex social issues. Organizations and governments are increasingly turning to AI to enhance disaster response, improve healthcare delivery, and optimize resource allocation in impoverished communities. AI-powered chatbots are being used to provide mental health support to individuals in crisis, while predictive analytics are helping food banks better anticipate and meet the needs of vulnerable populations. These applications demonstrate the potential of AI to drive positive change and improve the well-being of society at large. AI for social good initiatives are playing a key role in advancing the United Nations Sustainable Development Goals by leveraging technology to tackle poverty, promote health and well-being, and combat climate change. By harnessing the power of AI, organizations are able to analyze vast amounts of data in real-time, identify trends, and implement targeted interventions that can significantly impact the lives of individuals in need. From disaster preparedness to refugee assistance, AI is proving to be a valuable tool in building more resilient and sustainable communities around the world. Despite the undeniable potential of AI for social good, it is essential to approach these initiatives with caution and foresight. As AI systems become more sophisticated, ethical considerations surrounding issues such as transparency, accountability, and bias become increasingly important. It is crucial for organizations to prioritize ethical guidelines and regulatory frameworks that ensure the responsible deployment of AI technologies in humanitarian contexts. By promoting transparency, inclusivity, and participatory decision-making, we can maximize the benefits of AI while minimizing potential risks and unintended consequences for vulnerable populations.

Data-driven decision-making in philanthropic efforts

In philanthropic efforts, data-driven decision-making plays a crucial role in maximizing impact and efficiency. By leveraging data analytics, philanthropic organizations can identify trends, assess needs, and measure outcomes more accurately than ever before. By analyzing demographic data and social indicators, foundations can target their resources towards areas with the greatest need, ensuring that their interventions have a lasting and meaningful impact. Data-driven decision-making can also help philanthropic organizations track progress over time, enabling them to refine their strategies and allocate resources more effectively. Data-driven decision-making in philanthropy can foster greater transparency and accountability. By collecting and analyzing data on how funds are being utilized and what results are being achieved, organizations can demonstrate their impact to donors, stakeholders, and the public. This transparency not only builds trust and credibility but also allows for greater collaboration and partnership within the sector. Through data-driven decision-making, philanthropic organizations can make informed choices that align with their mission and values, ultimately leading to more sustainable and impactful outcomes for the communities they serve. It is essential to recognize the limitations and challenges of data-driven decision-making in philanthropy. While data analytics can provide valuable insights, it is not a panacea and must be complemented by human judgment, empathy, and context. Philanthropy is inherently complex, dealing with issues of social justice, equity, and human welfare that cannot always be quantified or measured through data alone. While data-driven decision-making can enhance efficiency and effectiveness, it must be balanced with a nuanced understanding of the social, cultural, and ethical dimensions of philanthropic work. Successful philanthropy requires a holistic approach that integrates data analytics with human wisdom and compassion.

Ensuring equity and inclusivity in AI-driven social impact projects

In the realm of AI-driven social impact projects, ensuring equity and inclusivity is paramount to avoid exacerbating existing disparities. One key aspect to consider is the data used to train AI algorithms, as biased or incomplete datasets can result in discriminatory outcomes. It is crucial to ensure that training data is representative of diverse populations to avoid reinforcing societal inequalities. Transparency in the AI development process is essential to allow for scrutiny and accountability. By making algorithms and decision-making processes open to public review, stakeholders can identify and address biases before they result in harmful consequences. Promoting diversity in the teams developing AI technologies is vital for creating solutions that benefit all members of society. Including individuals from diverse backgrounds can help in challenging assumptions and biases that may be ingrained in the technology. Engaging with communities that will be impacted by AI-driven projects is essential to incorporate their perspectives and ensure that solutions are tailored to their needs. By fostering collaboration and co-creation, the development of AI technologies can be guided by a broader range of voices, leading to more inclusive outcomes. Proactive measures must be taken to ensure that AI-driven social impact projects are designed with equity and inclusivity in mind. This requires a commitment to diversity in both data collection and algorithm development, as well as engaging with communities affected by these technologies. By centering ethical considerations and prioritizing social responsibility, we can harness the potential of AI to address societal challenges while minimizing harm. By fostering a culture of inclusivity and fairness in AI development, we can work towards a future where advanced technologies benefit all members of society.

XXX. AI IN ENTERTAINMENT AND MEDIA

Advances in AI have significantly impacted the entertainment and media industries, revolutionizing the way content is created, distributed, and consumed. AI algorithms are increasingly being used to personalize recommendations for music, movies, and news content, enhancing user experience and engagement. Streaming platforms like Netflix leverage AI to analyze viewing habits and preferences to suggest relevant content to users, leading to increased viewer satisfaction and retention. In the realm of gaming, AI-powered technologies are utilized to create realistic characters, improve gameplay mechanics, and even generate dynamic storylines, offering players a more immersive and customized experience. AI is transforming the production process in the entertainment industry, streamlining tasks such as scriptwriting, video editing, and special effects creation. Machine learning algorithms can analyze vast amounts of data to predict audience preferences, optimize marketing strategies, and even forecast box office performance, enabling studios to make informed decisions and maximize their impact. AI-driven tools like virtual influencers and deepfake technologies are blurring the lines between reality and fiction, raising ethical concerns regarding authenticity and misinformation. As AI continues to evolve, it is essential for content creators and platforms to prioritize ethics and transparency to maintain trust and credibility with their audiences. While AI offers immense potential for innovation and efficiency in the entertainment and media sectors, it also poses challenges related to privacy, data security, and societal impact. The collection and analysis of user data by

AI algorithms raise concerns about privacy breaches and potential misuse of personal information. The reliance on AI for content curation and recommendation algorithms may lead to filter bubbles and echo chambers, limiting exposure to diverse perspectives and contributing to the spread of misinformation. As AI technologies become more prevalent in shaping media consumption habits, there is a growing need for regulations and ethical guidelines to ensure accountability, safeguard user privacy, and promote a fair and inclusive media landscape.

AI-driven content creation in the entertainment industry

In the entertainment industry, AI-driven content creation is revolutionizing the way stories are told and experiences are designed. From generating plotlines to designing virtual worlds, AI is pushing the boundaries of creativity and innovation. By analyzing vast amounts of data and identifying patterns, AI systems can predict audience preferences and tailor content to specific demographics. This not only streamlines the creative process but also enhances the overall viewer experience by delivering personalized and engaging entertainment. AI-driven content creation has the potential to democratize the entertainment industry, giving aspiring creators access to powerful tools and resources that were once exclusive to established studios. By leveraging AI algorithms, independent filmmakers, game developers, and artists can enhance their storytelling capabilities and reach a wider audience. This democratization can lead to a more diverse and inclusive entertainment landscape, showcasing a variety of voices and perspectives that may have been overlooked in traditional media. As AI continues to play a larger role in content creation, ethical considerations must be carefully addressed. The potential for AI to perpetuate biases, manipulate emotions, or infringe on privacy raises important questions about the ethical boundaries of AI-driven entertainment. Striking a balance between innovation and responsibility is crucial to ensure that AI is used ethically and to benefit society as a whole. By developing robust ethical guidelines and regulations, the entertainment industry can harness the power of AI to create captivating and thought-provoking content while upholding values of fairness, transparency, and respect for individual rights.

Personalized recommendations and content curation using AI algorithms

One of the remarkable applications of AI algorithms is in personalized recommendations and content curation. By leveraging machine learning techniques, these algorithms analyze vast amounts of data to understand user preferences and behaviors, allowing for tailored suggestions. Platforms like Netflix and Amazon utilize AI to recommend movies or products based on a users viewing or purchasing history. This not only enhances user experience by providing relevant content but also increases engagement and customer satisfaction. The ability of AI algorithms to continuously learn and adapt to individual preferences is reshaping the way content is consumed, offering a more personalized and streamlined experience. Content curation powered by AI algorithms is revolutionizing the way information is presented to users. In the era of information overload, these algorithms play a crucial role in filtering and organizing content based on relevance and interest. Social media platforms like Facebook use AI to curate news feeds, showing users content that aligns with their interests and interactions. This not only saves users time by presenting them with content they are likely to engage with but also helps in combating misinformation by promoting reliable sources. The efficiency and accuracy of AI algorithms in content curation are key factors in improving the quality of information consumed by users in a digital world inundated with content. Despite the numerous benefits of personalized recommendations and content curation using AI algorithms, there are challenges and ethical considerations that need to be addressed. Concerns around privacy, bias in recommendation systems, and the potential for manipulation underscore the importance of implementing transparent and accountable practices. As AI continues to evolve and impact various aspects of our lives, it is crucial to establish guidelines and regulations that uphold ethical standards and protect user rights. Striking a balance between harnessing the capabilities of AI for personalized experiences and safeguarding user privacy and autonomy is essential for building trust and acceptance of these technologies in society.

Ethical considerations in AI-generated media content
One crucial aspect to consider in the realm of AI-generated media content is the ethical implications that come with the creation and distribution of such material. As AI becomes more advanced and capable of producing incredibly lifelike images, videos, and texts, questions arise regarding consent, privacy, and authenticity. Deepfake technology can be used to manipulate videos to make it appear as though individuals are saying or doing things they never actually did. This raises concerns about

the potential for misinformation, defamation, and even black-mail. Ethical considerations surrounding the use of AI in media content creation are paramount in ensuring that such technologies are deployed responsibly and do not harm individuals or society as a whole. Transparency in the development and deployment of AI-generated content is essential for building trust with the public. Users should be aware when they are interacting with content generated by AI, as this can have implications for how they perceive and trust the information presented to them. From news articles to social media posts, the use of AI in generating content requires clear labeling and disclosure to prevent misleading audiences. The algorithms and datasets used in creating AI-generated media must be scrutinized to ensure they are free from biases that could perpetuate harmful stereotypes or misinformation. By implementing ethical guidelines and transparency measures, the potential risks associated with AI-generated media content can be mitigated. In light of the ethical considerations surrounding AI-generated media content, it is imperative that a regulatory framework is established to govern its development and use. Industry standards and guidelines can help ensure that AI technologies are developed and deployed in a manner that upholds ethical principles and respects individual rights. By holding developers and organizations accountable for the content created by AI systems, regulatory bodies can help safeguard against potential abuses and promote responsible use of these technologies. Ethical considerations in AI-generated media content are crucial for shaping a future in which technology advances in a way that benefits society as a whole, while upholding fundamental values and principles.

XXXI. AI IN FINANCIAL SERVICES

In the realm of financial services, AI has become a game-changer, revolutionizing how institutions handle data analysis, risk assessment, and customer interactions. Machine learning algorithms can process vast amounts of financial information at lightning speed, enabling more accurate predictions and real-time decision-making. Natural language processing systems can scan news articles and social media to gauge market sentiment, helping traders make informed choices. AI-powered chatbots are being used for customer service, providing personalized assistance and enhancing user experience. The integration of AI in financial services streamlines operations, reduces costs, and ultimately improves efficiency and overall performance. The implementation of AI in financial institutions has raised concerns about data privacy and security. With access to sensitive personal and financial data, there is a heightened risk of cyberattacks and breaches. As AI systems become more sophisticated, ensuring robust cybersecurity measures is crucial to protect both the institutions and their clients. The use of AI algorithms in decision-making processes, such as loan approvals or investment recommendations, prompts a discussion about transparency and accountability. It is imperative for financial organizations to maintain transparency in how AI algorithms operate and the factors they consider in making decisions. Ethical considerations must be at the forefront to prevent biases and discrimination in financial services driven by AI. Despite the undeniable benefits of AI in financial services, there are concerns about its potential to disrupt the job market. As AI automates routine tasks and data analysis, there is a risk of job displacement for roles that can be easily replaced by machines. This also presents an opportunity for upskilling the workforce to focus on higher-value tasks that require critical thinking and creativity. Financial institutions need to invest in training programs to equip employees with the skills necessary to collaborate effectively with AI systems. Policymakers must address the implications of AI on employment and develop strategies to support workers through re-skilling initiatives and job transitions. By embracing AI responsibly and proactively addressing its impacts on the workforce, the financial services industry can navigate the challenges and harness the full potential of AI innovation.

AI applications in fraud detection and risk management

In the realm of fraud detection and risk management, AI is revolutionizing the way organizations protect themselves from financial losses and potential threats. Through the use of sophisticated algorithms and machine learning capabilities, AI systems can analyze vast amounts of data in real-time, detecting patterns and anomalies that may indicate fraudulent activities. This proactive approach enables companies to respond swiftly to potential risks, safeguarding their operations and assets. By leveraging AI technologies, organizations can enhance their fraud detection methods, minimizing the impact of fraudulent behavior on their bottom line. AI applications in fraud detection and risk management can significantly reduce the burden on human analysts, allowing them to focus on more complex tasks that require human intervention. These systems can autonomously monitor transactions, identify suspicious activities, and even predict future risks based on historical patterns. By streamlining the detection process and providing timely alerts, AI empowers organizations to take proactive measures to mitigate potential threats before they escalate. As a result, companies can operate more efficiently and effectively, safeguarding their financial integrity and reputation in an increasingly complex and interconnected business environment. The integration of AI in fraud detection and risk management represents a significant advancement in the field, offering organizations powerful tools to combat financial crimes and mitigate potential risks. By harnessing the capabilities of AI systems to analyze data in real-time, organizations can strengthen their defenses against fraud and make informed decisions to protect their assets. As AI technologies continue to evolve and improve, they will play an increasingly vital role in helping organizations stay ahead of emerging threats and adapt to the dynamic landscape of digital commerce. Embracing the potential of AI in fraud detection and risk management is essential for businesses seeking to secure their future in an era of rapid technological advancement.

Algorithmic trading and predictive analytics in finance

Algorithmic trading and predictive analytics have revolutionized the financial industry, enabling institutions to make data-driven decisions at lightning speed. By using complex mathematical algorithms, these systems can analyze vast amounts of historical and real-time data to predict market trends and optimize trading strategies. This technology has significantly reduced the reliance on human judgment, leading to increased efficiency and profitability in trading operations. The rise of algorithmic trading has also raised concerns about market manipulation and the potential for unforeseen consequences in the event of system failures or glitches. One of the key advantages of algorithmic trading is its ability to process information and execute trades much faster than any human trader could. This speed advantage allows firms to capitalize on fleeting opportunities in the market, giving them a competitive edge. Predictive analytics can help identify patterns and correlations in data that human analysts may overlook, leading to more accurate predictions of market movements. Despite these benefits, the increasing complexity of algorithms raises questions about transparency and accountability in the financial markets. As algorithms become more sophisticated, regulators and investors must grapple with ensuring that these systems are used ethically and in compliance with regulations. As algorithmic trading and predictive analytics continue to reshape the financial landscape, it is crucial for market participants to adapt to this technological shift. Traders and financial professionals must develop new skills to leverage these tools effectively and mitigate risks associated with automated trading systems. Regulators must establish clear guidelines and oversight mechanisms to ensure that algorithmic trading does not pose systemic risks to the financial system. By embracing innovation while maintaining a cautious approach, the financial industry can harness the power of algorithmic trading and predictive analytics to drive growth and efficiency in a rapidly evolving market environment.

Regulatory challenges and transparency in AI-driven financial decisions

In the realm of AI-driven financial decisions, one of the primary challenges lies in the regulatory landscape that governs the use of these technologies. As AI becomes more ingrained in the financial sector, there is a growing need for clear guidelines and standards to ensure transparency and accountability. Without robust regulations, there is a risk of potential biases, errors, or even malicious intent influencing AI algorithms, leading to adverse outcomes in financial decision-making. Policymakers and regulators must work in tandem with industry experts to establish frameworks that not only promote innovation but also safeguard against the misuse of AI in financial settings. Transparency is another crucial aspect that must be addressed when it comes to AI-driven financial decisions. Given the complexity of machine learning algorithms and the vast amounts of data involved, it can be challenging for individuals to understand how decisions are being made. This lack of transparency can lead to mistrust and skepticism regarding the outcomes of AI-driven financial models. To address this issue, companies utilizing AI in finance must prioritize transparency by providing explanations of how algorithms reach conclusions and making efforts to demystify the decision-making process. By doing so, they can build trust with consumers and stakeholders while also ensuring that AI is used responsibly and ethically in financial contexts. In navigating the regulatory challenges and transparency issues surrounding AI-driven financial decisions, collaboration among various stakeholders is essential. Industry leaders, regulators, policymakers, and ethicists must come together to establish a cohesive framework that balances innovation with accountability. By fostering open dialogue and cooperation, it is possible to create regulations that support the responsible use of AI in finance while also promoting transparency in decision-making processes. By addressing these issues head-on, the financial

sector can harness the transformative power of AI while upholding ethical standards and ensuring that decisions are made in
the best interest of all stakeholders involved.

XXXII. AI IN HUMANITARIAN AID AND CRISIS RESPONSE

AI is also proving to be a valuable tool in humanitarian aid and crisis response. Machine learning algorithms can analyze vast amounts of data to predict and prevent disasters, as well as assist in delivering aid more efficiently. During natural disasters, AI can help identify areas most in need of assistance based on satellite imagery and real-time data. This can streamline the distribution of resources and maximize the impact of relief efforts. Chatbots powered by AI can provide support and information to victims, helping to alleviate stress and connect them with the necessary services. AI technology is being used to optimize supply chains and logistics in humanitarian aid operations. By predicting demand and tracking inventory in real-time, organizations can ensure that resources reach those in need promptly. AI-powered drones can also deliver aid to remote or inaccessible areas, reducing response times and overall costs. These advancements not only improve the effectiveness of humanitarian missions but also enhance the safety of aid workers in challenging environments. It is crucial to address ethical concerns, such as data privacy and the potential for bias in AI decision-making, to ensure that these technologies serve the greater good without causing harm or discrimination. The integration of AI in humanitarian aid and crisis response demonstrates the positive impact that advanced technologies can have on society. By harnessing the power of AI for predictive analytics, resource allocation, and logistics management, humanitarian organizations can enhance their efficiency and effectiveness in delivering aid to those in need. It is essential to approach these developments with caution and a strong ethical frame-work to mitigate potential risks and ensure that AI serves to benefit all individuals, especially in times of crisis. As we con-tinue to advance towards the technological singularity, it is im-perative to leverage AI responsibly to create a more sustainable and equitable future for humanity.

AI for disaster relief coordination and resource allocation

In the realm of disaster relief coordination and resource alloca-tion, AI holds immense promise for enhancing response efforts. By leveraging machine learning algorithms and real-time data analysis, AI systems can swiftly assess the extent of a disaster, identify areas in dire need of assistance, and optimize the allo-cation of resources. AI-powered drones can be deployed to sur-vey affected areas, provide critical information to response teams, and deliver supplies to hard-to-reach locations. This level of efficiency and precision can significantly expedite relief operations, ultimately saving more lives and mitigating the im-pact of catastrophes. AI-enabled predictive modeling can fore-cast potential disasters and anticipate their consequences, en-abling preemptive measures to be taken. By analyzing historical data and environmental patterns, AI algorithms can identify high-risk areas susceptible to floods, droughts, or other natural phenomena. This foresight empowers authorities to implement preventive measures, evacuate at-risk populations, and stock-pile resources in advance, thereby reducing the severity of future disasters. AI systems can continuously adapt and learn from new data inputs, improving their predictive capabilities over time and enhancing the overall resilience of communities to potential crises. Despite its potential benefits, the integration of AI in disaster relief raises ethical considerations regarding data privacy, algorithmic bias, and decision-making autonomy. As AI systems become increasingly autonomous in resource allocation and decision-making processes, there is a need for transparent protocols and accountability mechanisms to ensure fair and equitable outcomes. The reliance on AI technologies must be complemented by human expertise and ethical oversight to prevent unintended consequences or discriminatory practices. By striking a balance between AI automation and human intervention, disaster response efforts can harness the full potential of AI while upholding ethical standards and safeguarding the rights of those affected by emergencies.

Predictive analytics for early warning systems in humanitarian crises

In the context of the technological singularity, the application of predictive analytics for early warning systems in humanitarian crises represents a crucial advancement. By harnessing the power of AI and machine learning algorithms, organizations can now forecast potential crises before they unfold, enabling timely intervention and mitigation strategies. These systems can analyze vast amounts of data, such as weather patterns, population movements, and social media trends, to identify early indicators of a crisis. This proactive approach not only saves lives but also reduces the overall impact on affected communities. Predictive analytics can significantly improve resource allocation during humanitarian crises. By accurately predicting the onset and severity of disasters, aid organizations can strategically position supplies, personnel, and infrastructure to respond effectively. This optimization of resources ensures a swifter and more targeted response, ultimately increasing the efficiency and effectiveness of relief efforts. By leveraging historical data and real-time information, predictive analytics can enhance decision-making processes, enabling organizations to adapt their strategies based on evolving circumstances. Predictive analytics for early warning systems in humanitarian crises have the potential to revolutionize the way we address disasters and mitigate their impact. As we navigate towards the technological singularity, integrating AI-driven solutions into humanitarian operations becomes paramount. By embracing these advanced technologies and fostering collaboration between human expertise and machine intelligence, we can build more resilient communities and improve our ability to respond to crises with agility and precision. It is essential for stakeholders to invest in the development and implementation of predictive analytics to ensure that we are prepared to face the challenges of the future.

Ethical considerations in using AI for humanitarian efforts

When considering the use of AI for humanitarian efforts, it is imperative to address the ethical implications that arise. One of the main concerns is the potential for bias in AI algorithms, which can perpetuate discrimination and inequality in the services provided. In healthcare, AI systems may inadvertently favor certain demographics over others, leading to unequal access to medical resources. It is crucial to develop AI technologies that are transparent, accountable, and unbiased, to ensure fair and equitable outcomes for all individuals in need of assistance. Another important ethical consideration is the protection of privacy and data security when deploying AI in humanitarian settings. As AI systems collect and process vast amounts of personal information, there is a risk of data breaches and misuse that could compromise the safety and well-being of vulnerable populations. Striking a balance between leveraging data for effective decision-making and safeguarding individuals privacy rights is essential to maintain trust and uphold ethical standards in AI-driven humanitarian initiatives. By implementing robust data protection measures and ensuring transparency in data usage, organizations can mitigate these risks and uphold the principles of respect for individuals autonomy and dignity. While the potential benefits of using AI for humanitarian efforts are significant, it is essential to navigate the ethical considerations associated with deploying these technologies responsibly. By prioritizing fairness, transparency, and data protection in the development and implementation of AI systems, organizations can ensure that their humanitarian initiatives uphold ethical standards and contribute positively to the well-being of communities in need. By fostering a culture of ethical AI use, we can harness the power of technology to address global challenges in a way that respects and protects the rights and dignity of all individuals.

XXXIII. CONCLUSION

In considering the implications of the technological singularity and the rise of higher AI, it becomes clear that society must be proactive in shaping the future landscape. The convergence of AI, automation, and machine learning signals a significant shift in how industries operate, posing both opportunities and challenges. As we stand on the precipice of this transformative era, it is imperative that we establish a robust ethical framework to govern the development and deployment of these advanced technologies. This framework should prioritize accountability, fairness, and transparency to ensure that AI serves the greater good and mitigates potential risks. The readiness of society to transition towards higher AI must be evaluated in terms of education and job readiness. The current workforce will require upskilling and retraining to adapt to the changing demands of the job market in a more automated world. Educational systems must evolve to cultivate a workforce equipped with both technical expertise and critical thinking skills, enabling individuals to collaborate effectively with AI systems. By investing in education and training programs that focus on AI literacy and skill development, societies can better prepare for the disruptions and opportunities that advanced AI will bring. As we navigate the complexities of the technological singularity, it is essential to consider the broader implications for employment and the economy. The potential for mass unemployment due to automation raises significant concerns about income inequality and social stability. Policymakers must be proactive in implementing measures that support displaced workers, such as retraining initiatives and social safety nets. Strategies to stimulate job creation in emerging sectors that leverage AI technology can help mitigate the negative impacts of automation on the labor market. By fostering a supportive environment for human-AI collaboration, societies can harness the transformative power of AI while ensuring that its benefits are equitably distributed across the population.

BIBLIOGRAPHY

Jyh-An Lee. 'Artificial Intelligence and Intellectual Property.' Reto Hilty, Oxford University Press, 2/25/2021

Jaxon Emberwood. 'AI-Powered Content Creation.' Scaling Your Marketing Efforts with Automated Content Generation, Amazon Digital Services LLC - Kdp, 2/28/2024

Arthur I. Miller. 'The Artist in the Machine.' The World of AI-Powered Creativity, MIT Press, 11/10/2020

Ilee DeSoto. 'The Art of Algorithms.' Exploring AI in Creative Industries, eBookIt.com, 3/21/2024

Madalina Busuioc. 'Chapter 31: AI algorithmic oversight: new frontiers in regulation.' Edward Elgar Publishing, 1/1/2022

Ben Adams. 'Law in the Age of Artificial Intelligence.' Navigating Legal Frontiers in an Evolving Technological Landscape, Amazon Digital Services LLC - Kdp, 4/2/2024

Sid Ahmed Benraouane. 'AI Management System Certification According to the ISO/IEC 42001 Standard.' How to Audit, Certify, and Build Responsible AI Systems, CRC Press, 6/24/2024

Brian Ka Chan. 'Artificial Intelligence Governance.' A Primer of AI Governance and Regulation, Independently Published, 12/24/2017

Woodrow Barfield. 'The Cambridge Handbook of the Law of Algorithms.' Cambridge University Press, 11/5/2020

Petar Radanliev. 'Beyond the Algorithm.' AI, Security, Privacy, and Ethics, Omar Santos, Addison-Wesley Professional, 1/30/2024

Lakshitha Rikhab Chand Jain. 'A Comprehensive Study of Algorithmic Bias : Fairness in AI, Ethical and Social Implications in Real World Applications.' A Thesis, University of Alabama in Huntsville, 1/1/2023

Arnold Villeneuve. 'Ethical AI Coding.' Navigating the Moral Landscape of AI Development, Amazon Digital Services LLC - Kdp, 3/19/2024

Joseph F. Paris Jr.. 'State of Readiness.' Operational Excellence as Precursor to Becoming a High-Performance Organization, Greenleaf Book Group, 5/16/2017

Charles Morgan. 'Responsible AI.' A Global Policy Framework, International Technology Law Association, 1/1/2019

Joseph McCormack. 'Brief.' Make a Bigger Impact by Saying Less, John Wiley & Sons, 2/10/2014

Dariusz Jemielniak. 'Strategizing AI in Business and Education.' Emerging Technologies and Business Strategy, Aleksandra Przegalinska, Cambridge University Press, 4/6/2023

David A. Mindell. 'The Work of the Future.' Building Better Jobs in an Age of Intelligent Machines, David H. Autor, MIT Press, 10/3/2023

William Welser IV. 'An Intelligence in Our Image.' The Risks of Bias and Errors in Artificial Intelligence, Osonde A. Osoba, Rand Corporation, 4/5/2017

OECD. 'Artificial Intelligence in Society.' OECD Publishing, 6/11/2019

UNESCO International Centre for Technical and Vocational Education and Training. 'Understanding the impact of AI on skills development.' UNESCO Publishing, 4/2/2021

William B. Weeks. 'AI for Good.' Applications in Sustainability, Humanitarian Action, and Health, Juan M. Lavista Ferres, John Wiley & Sons, 1/23/2024

Richard J Wallace. 'Artificial Intelligence/ Human Intelligence: An Indissoluble Nexus.' World Scientific, 3/2/2021

Ray Kurzweil. 'The Singularity Is Nearer.' When We Merge with AI, Penguin, 6/25/2024

Arnold Villeneuve. 'The Future of AI Governance.' Balancing Innovation and Ethical Responsibility, Amazon Digital Services LLC - Kdp, 3/22/2024

Malik Ghallab. 'Reflections on Artificial Intelligence for Humanity.' Bertrand Braunschweig, Springer Nature, 2/6/2021

Timo Rademacher. 'Regulating Artificial Intelligence.' Thomas Wischmeyer, Springer Nature, 11/29/2019

Robert M. Schumacher Jr.. 'AI and UX.' Why Artificial Intelligence Needs User Experience, Gavin Lew, Apress, 10/17/2020

Steven M. Miller. 'Working with AI.' Real Stories of Human-Machine Collaboration, Thomas H. Davenport, MIT Press, 9/27/2022

Readyai. 'Human-AI Interaction.' How We Work with Artificial Intelligence, Indy Pub, 1/25/2021

Division on Engineering and Physical Sciences. 'Implications of Artificial Intelligence for Cybersecurity.' Proceedings of a Workshop, National Academies of Sciences, Engineering, and Medicine, National Academies Press, 1/27/2020

John T. Addison. 'Job Displacement.' Consequences and Implications for Policy, Wayne State University Press, 1/1/1991

Nikhil Jain. 'Advances in Smart Healthcare Paradigms and Applications.' Outstanding Women in Healthcare—Volume 1, Halina Kwaśnicka, Springer Nature, 8/16/2023

Joachim Funke. 'Complex Problem Solving.' The European Perspective, Peter A. Frensch, Psychology Press, 4/4/2014

Christopher Oosthuisen. 'Mastering Efficiency and Productivity.' How to Run Your Life and Business Like a Billion Dollar Company, Independently Published, 1/30/2020

Johnny Ch LOK. 'Artificial Intelligence Brings Advantages Or Disadvantages.' To Impact Human Job Market, Independently Published, 4/1/2018

Bernd Carsten Stahl. 'Artificial Intelligence for a Better Future.' An Ecosystem Perspective on the Ethics of AI and Emerging Digital Technologies, Springer Nature, 3/17/2021

Kaveh Memarzadeh. 'Artificial Intelligence in Healthcare.' Adam Bohr, Academic Press, 6/21/2020

Christoph Lütge. 'An Introduction to Ethics in Robotics and AI.' Christoph Bartneck, Springer Nature, 8/11/2020

National Science and on Technology. 'Preparing for the Future of Artificial Intelligence.' A Government Report, Executive Office President, CreateSpace Independent Publishing Platform, 3/12/2017

Alexandra C. Norkin. 'Thesis Statement.' Wellesley College., 1/1/1976

Michael Wooldridge. 'A Brief History of Artificial Intelligence.' What It Is, Where We Are, and Where We Are Going, Flatiron Books, 1/19/2021

Ray Kurzweil. 'The Singularity Is Near.' When Humans Transcend Biology, Penguin, 9/22/2005

www.ingramcontent.com/pod-product-compliance
Lightning Source LLC
Chambersburg PA
CBHW071829210526
45479CB00001B/49